Excel GRAMMAR AND PUNCTUATION WORKBOOK

ADVANCED SKILLS

ENGLISH YEAR 6 AGES 11–12

Get the Results You Want!

PASCAL PRESS

Laura Anderson

© 2013 Laura Anderson and Pascal Press
Reprinted 2015, 2016

ISBN 978 1 74125 402 0

Pascal Press
PO Box 250
Glebe NSW 2037
(02) 8585 4044
www.pascalpress.com.au

Publisher: Vivienne Joannou
Project editors: Mark Dixon and Leanne Poll
Edited by Leanne Howard
Reviewed by Dale Little and Kristine Brown
Cover and page design by DiZign Pty Ltd
Typeset by lj Design (Julianne Billington)
Printed by Green Giant Press

Reproduction and communication for educational purposes
The Australian *Copyright Act 1968* (the Act) allows a maximum of one chapter or 10% of the pages of this work, whichever is the greater, to be reproduced and/or communicated by any educational institution for its educational purposes provided that the educational institution (or the body that administers it) has given a remuneration notice to Copyright Agency Limited (CAL) under the Act.

For details of the CAL licence for educational institutions contact:

Copyright Agency Limited
Level 15, 233 Castlereagh Street
Sydney NSW 2000
Telephone: (02) 9394 7600
Facsimile: (02) 9394 7601
Email: enquiry@copyright.com.au

Reproduction and communication for other purposes
Except as permitted under the Act (for example, a fair dealing for the purposes of study, research, criticism or review) no part of this book may be reproduced, stored in a retrieval system, communicated or transmitted in any form or by any means without prior written permission. All inquiries should be made to the publisher at the address above.

All efforts to contact individuals regarding copyright have been made and permission acknowledged where applicable. In the event of any oversight, please contact the publisher so correction can be made in subsequent editions.

Contents

To the student v

About this book vi

Unit 1 Epic journeys 1
Factual recounts
Nouns 1
Capital letters 1

Unit 2 A whale of a time! 7
Personal recounts/narratives
Pronouns 7

Unit 3 Chocolate 13
Factual recounts/magazine articles
Adjectives 13

Unit 4 Shipwrecks 19
Website articles/emails
Verbs 19
Verb groups 21

Unit 5 We're going camping! 25
Narratives
Sentences 25
Subjects and predicates 27

Unit 6 Courage 31
Website articles
Verbal adjectives 31
Verbal nouns 33

Unit 7 Greek mythology 37
Myths
Adverbs 37

Unit 8 Chew on this! 43
Information leaflets
Conjunctions 43
Prepositions 45

Unit 9 Striking it rich! 49
Explanations/factual recounts
Adjectival and adverbial phrases 49
Noun phrases 51
Commas 51

Unit 10 Natural disasters 55
Descriptions/factual recounts
Sentences: subjects, verbs and objects 55
Active and passive voice 57

Unit 11 Robots **61**
Discussions/recounts
Direct speech 61
Speech marks 61
Indirect speech 63

Unit 12 Animals with armour **67**
Information reports
Clauses: simple, compound and complex sentences 67

Unit 13 Famous Australians **73**
Responses/biographies
Quotation marks and colons 73
Brackets and abbreviations 75

Unit 14 Acting it out **79**
Reviews/scripts
Adjectival and adverbial clauses and commas 79
Colons, brackets and ellipses 81

Unit 15 Changing fashions **85**
Diary entries/descriptions
Apostrophes that show contractions 85
Apostrophes that show ownership 87

Unit 16 Rules and regulations **91**
Expositions
Modality and adverbs 91
Nominalisation 93

Unit 17 Television **97**
Debates/advertisements
Evaluative language 97
Emotive language 99

Unit 18 Time **103**
Poems
Figures of speech: similes and metaphors 103
Personification 105

Glossary of terms **109**

Answers **111**

To the student

This book explains the rules of grammar and punctuation that you need for Year 6.

Each unit focuses on two or more grammar rules. Before each rule is explained, there is a text that lets you see how the rule works in everyday writing. These texts are important as they are models of the different text types and will help you in your own writing. At the end of each unit there is also a short, NAPLAN-style test that lets you see how well you have understood the grammar rules.

Most of the activities can be written in this book, but you will have to use your own paper for the writing activity at the end of each unit. I suggest you buy a notebook or folder for this. The writing activities are very important. The more you do, the faster your English will improve. If you are not sure how to write something, use the example texts as a model.

It is important that you work through this book from Unit 1 to the end. This will help you build your skills and become a more confident speaker and writer of English. Make sure that you understand the work in each unit before you go on to the next one. Remember to have a dictionary handy as you work through the book, and to ask for help if you need it. There is a glossary on pages 109–110 at the end of the book that explains the grammatical terms used in the units.

I hope you enjoy reading the texts and doing all the activities.

Good luck!

Laura Anderson

About this book

This book consists of eighteen units, each covering one or more aspects of grammar or punctuation. Each unit is theme-based and contains two texts designed to introduce the grammatical features and to show students how they function in context. These are followed by detailed explanations of how and why the grammar features are used, as well as exercises that allow students to put the knowledge they have acquired into practice. As an aid to revision, there is a glossary at the end of the book that summarises the grammatical terms used in the units.

The exercises in the units are organised as follows:

Let's find them!
- These exercises require students to find examples of the grammatical feature in question in the texts. They are straightforward exercises designed to test recall.

Let's go to the next step!
- This set of exercises is more difficult, requiring students to apply the knowledge they have acquired.

Let's aim high now!
- These are challenging exercises, again requiring students to apply what they have learnt.

Let's put it all together now!
- This is an editing exercise designed to test the students' understanding of the material covered in the whole unit. It also acts as a revision exercise.

Let's have fun!
- Although this exercise is designed to be fun, it is also challenging. It reinforces the material learnt.

Let's have a test!
- This series of eight NAPLAN-style questions helps students revise for the NAPLAN Tests and also tests their knowledge of the material learnt in the unit as a whole. The questions are graded so that they increase in difficulty.

Let's write now!
- This activity encourages students to write their own text in which they use the grammar and punctuation they have learnt in the unit. The texts are based on the theme and text types featured in the unit.

Most of the exercises in this book consist of seven questions, as we believe they give students the practice they need to fully grasp the rules of grammar and punctuation.

Unit 1 Epic journeys

Focus
Nouns; capital letters

Marco Polo's journey to China

More than 700 years ago, Marco **Polo** completed one of the most epic journeys in history. At that time, the Europeans and the Chinese knew very little about each other. Their lands were separated by vast **deserts** and mountain ranges, making travel between the two regions difficult.

Marco Polo was born in Venice, which is today a **city** in Italy. In 1271, Marco set out with his father and uncle for China. They made their way through **countries** like **Armenia**, Persia and Afghanistan, and crossed the **Pamir Mountains** and Gobi Desert in Central Asia before arriving at the court of Kublai Khan, the Mongolian ruler of China. The journey took almost four years!

The **Polos** stayed in China for seventeen years. They arrived back in Venice in 1295, bringing with them many jewels. They also had wonderful stories to tell of the things they had seen and done in China.

by Ben

This is a **factual recount**. A recount tells about things that have already happened. Ben uses **common nouns** to name general people, places and things, and **proper nouns** to name particular people and places in his recount of the journey of Marco Polo.

Nouns are naming words. They name people, animals, places, things, qualities and feelings.

Common nouns
- name general people, animals, places and things; for example, **deserts**.
- do not start with a capital letter, unless they come at the beginning of the sentence.
- can be singular or plural; for example, **city**, **countries**.

Proper nouns
- name particular people, animals, places and things; for example, **Armenia**.
- always start with a **capital letter**.
- can be singular or plural; for example, **Polo**, **Polos**.

Let's find them!

Tip!
If a **proper noun** consists of two or more words, all of the words start with a **capital letter**; for example, Pamir Mountains.

Find these **common** and **proper nouns** in the text. Write the name of

1 sandy places _____

Unit 1: Epic journeys

② a particular sandy place _____

③ a person who is a family member _____

④ people who come from Europe _____

⑤ the place where Marco Polo was born _____

⑥ the things the Polos brought back with them from China _____

⑦ the ruler of China _____

Let's go to the next step!

Which **proper noun** does the underlined **common noun** in each sentence refer to? Choose the answer from the box.

For example: Marco Polo spent many years in this fascinating country. ___China___

Niccolo	Great Silk Road	Bass Strait
Queensland	Sahara	
January	Santa Maria	

① Christopher Columbus sailed to America in this <u>ship</u>. _____

② To this day, people cross this immense <u>desert</u> on camels. _____

③ Marco Polo's companions were his <u>father</u> and his uncle Maffeo. _____

④ Marco Polo died on the eighth or ninth day of this <u>month</u> in 1324. _____

⑤ This <u>channel</u> of water separates Tasmania from the rest of Australia. _____

⑥ Centuries ago, this was the main trade <u>route</u> between Europe and Asia. _____

⑦ Ludwig Leichhardt journeyed through parts of this Australian <u>state</u>. _____

Let's aim high now!

Use a red pen to show which words need **capital letters** in these sentences.

① the vikings, who came from scandinavia, sailed to iceland and greenland.

② in 1969 neil armstrong, buzz aldrin and michael collins journeyed to the moon.

③ christopher columbus' three ships were the nina, the pinta and the santa maria.

④ the botanist, joseph banks, accompanied captain james cook on his first voyage.

⑤ the norwegian, thor heyerdahl, sailed across the pacific ocean in a homemade raft.

⑥ charles darwin travelled to brazil, australia, the falkland islands and the galapagos islands.

⑦ there are many stories of epic journeys made by the ancient greeks, phoenicians egyptians and romans.

The race to the South Pole

Most people today know what Antarctica looks like. Thanks to the many documentaries on television, we've seen **colonies of penguins** waddling on its beaches. We've marvelled at pods of blue whales frolicking in its waters. We've watched flocks of birds flying above its icy landscape and, to cater for the tiny human population, clusters of little huts on its hillsides. But just over a hundred years ago, very little was known about this large, white continent.

At the beginning of the 20th century, Sir Robert Scott led an **expedition** onto the mainland of Antarctica. He received a hero's welcome when he returned to England. In 1910, he led a second expedition to the frozen continent, this time aiming to reach the South Pole. The expedition turned into a disaster. Struggling through harsh conditions, Scott's little party of five reached the South Pole on 17th January 1912, only to face **disappointment**. Roald Amundsen, the Norwegian, had beaten them to it. On the return journey, Scott and his men died of starvation and exposure.

by Rebecca

This is another **factual recount**. Rebecca uses **collective nouns** to name groups of people, animals and things, and **abstract nouns** to name things that we cannot see or touch in her recount of Robert Scott's expedition to the South Pole.

Collective nouns
- are the names of groups of people, animals or things; for example, **colonies** of **penguins**.
- can be singular or plural; for example, **colony** → **colonies**.

Abstract nouns name things that we cannot see or touch, such as feelings, qualities and other abstract ideas; for example, **expedition**, **disappointment**.

Let's find them!

Find these **collective** and **abstract** nouns in the text.
Write the name of

1. groups of whales _____
2. groups of huts _____
3. a group of men _____

Unit 1: **Epic journeys**   3

4. something Scott received on his return to England _____
5. something Scott's expedition turned into _____
6. something that was harsh _____
7. something that Scott and his men died of _____

Let's go to the next step!

Underline the **collective nouns** and circle the **abstract nouns** in these sentences. For example: Captain Cook and his <u>crew</u> set off on their first (expedition) in 1768.

1. Early explorers often turned to the local population for help.
2. Many early explorers wrote of the difficulty of crossing vast mountain ranges.
3. Robert Scott, an officer in the navy, is famous for his exploration of Antarctica.
4. The caravan stopped at an oasis where the travellers could quench their thirst.
5. The sailors commented on the beauty of the island, with its clusters of palm trees.
6. Roald Amundsen's team of dogs contributed to his success in reaching the South Pole.
7. Robert Scott's first appointment was as a midshipman on the flagship of a squadron of battleships.

Let's aim high now!

Complete these sentences by changing the words in brackets to **abstract nouns**. For example: The explorer said that his journey had been a great (adventurous) <u>adventure</u>.

1. Marco Polo faced many (dangerous) _____ on his journey to China.
2. Robert Scott and his men were suffering from (exhaust) _____.
3. Marco Polo wrote of his (excite) _____ at seeing strange lands.
4. Charles Darwin made many interesting (discover) _____ on the Galapagos Islands.
5. The explorer was close to (dead) _____ when a search party found him.
6. The explorers made careful (prepare) _____ before embarking on their journey.
7. The early explorers shared their (know) _____ of new lands with many people.

Let's put it together now!

This student has written two **common nouns**, two **proper nouns**, one **collective noun** and two **abstract nouns** incorrectly in this section of her recount. Use a red pen to make the corrections for her.

Matthew flinders was the first man to sail right around Australia. Amongst his Crew on the ship the *Investigator* was a botanist and two artist. He started his circumnavigation of the continent at the southern tip of western Australia in 1801. He headed in an easterly direct until he came to Port Phillip. His first impress of the land around Melbourne was that it looked fertile. Even though his Ship was leaking badly, he completed his circumnavigation of Australia on 9th June 1803.

Let's have fun!

The clues will help you complete this crossword puzzle. The answers are **common**, **proper**, **collective** or **abstract nouns**.

Across

1. Marco Polo passed through this country on his way to China.
4. Matthew Flinders' _____ around Australia took two years.
7. Robert Scott might have experienced this emotion of extreme fear in Antarctica.
8. Many sailors who travelled to Australia and New Zealand in the 18th and 19th centuries were in the British _____.
9. It must have taken great _____ to travel across the Asian continent 700 years ago!
10. The best animal to take with you on a journey through the desert is a _____.

Down

1. Marco Polo passed through this country on his way to China.
2. Many explorers journey long distances to find this precious metal.
3. Most explorers have a great sense of _____.
5. Marco Polo set out for China in the _____ 1271.
6. A _____ of horsemen escorted Marco Polo to Kublai Khan's court.
11. Some explorers might have used a _____ to find their way.

Unit 1: Epic journeys   5

Let's have a test!

1 Which sentence has been punctuated correctly?
- ○ David Livingstone journeyed through africa.
- ○ David livingstone journeyed through africa.
- ○ David Livingstone journeyed through Africa.
- ○ david livingstone journeyed through africa.

> **Tip!** Shade the circle with the correct answer

In questions 2–3, which words have been written **incorrectly**?

2 Matthew Flinders' Cat, Trim, accompanied him on his voyage around Australia.
- ○ Cat   ○ Trim   ○ voyage   ○ Australia

3 Captain James Cook spent a lot of time sailing around the Pacific ocean.
- ○ Cook   ○ time   ○ Pacific   ○ ocean

4 Which option replaces the underlined words correctly?

The explorer paddled down the <u>mighty river</u> in a canoe.
- ○ Amazon River   ○ Amazon river
- ○ amazon river   ○ amazon River

5 Which group of words is a list of collective nouns?
- ○ explorers, adventurers, travellers, sailors
- ○ party, crew, army, band
- ○ exploration, adventure, travel, voyage
- ○ China, Australia, Asia, Europe

6 Which option can best replace the underlined words?

A <u>group of men</u> at the Royal Society encouraged Robert Scott to explore Antarctica.
- ○ population   ○ pack   ○ committee   ○ choir

7 Which group of words is a list of abstract nouns?
- ○ anxiety, loyalty, dedication, bravery   ○ jury, troupe, staff, tribe
- ○ compass, mast, telescope, sled   ○ Scott, Polo, Flinders, Cook

8 Which suffix should be added to the word in brackets to turn it into an abstract noun?

Charles Darwin collected a lot of scientific (inform) on his journeys.
- ○ tion   ○ sion   ○ asion   ○ ation

Let's write now!

Find information on an explorer like Christopher Columbus or Charles Sturt who travelled long distances to find new lands. Write a **factual recount** about their experiences. Use **common**, **proper**, **collective** and **abstract nouns** in your recount.

Year 6 Grammar and Punctuation Workbook

Unit 2 — A whale of a time!

Focus: Pronouns

Whale watching

In the December school holidays **I** went with **my** family to Queensland. One of the most exciting things we did was to go whale watching.

We boarded our boat early in the morning and it wasn't long before we spotted a pod of humpback whales. They put on a great show for us. When two really big whales launched **themselves** out of the water, some of the others started slapping the surface with their fins, as though clapping for them. Everyone on the boat joined in. It was so funny!

We also saw dolphins and green turtles in the marine park. My dad, who regards himself as an expert on marine animals, reckons he spotted a loggerhead turtle as well, but no-one else saw it. I think Dad was having us on.

That day was the highlight of the holiday for me. You could say I had a whale of a time!

by Toby

This is a **personal recount**. A personal recount tells about things that have already happened. Toby uses **personal**, **possessive** and **reflexive pronouns** in place of common and proper nouns to avoid repeating nouns too often while telling about the time he went whale watching.

Personal pronouns are used in place of common and proper nouns; for example, **I** is used in place of Toby. **Possessive pronouns** are personal pronouns that show ownership; for example, **my** family.

Reflexive pronouns are personal pronouns that refer back to a common or proper noun or another pronoun; for example, **themselves** refers back to the noun *whales*.

These are the **personal pronouns**.

Singular	Plural
I, me	we, us
my, mine	our, ours
myself	ourselves
you	you
your, yours	your, yours
yourself	yourselves
he, him, she, her, it	they, them
his, her, hers, its	their, theirs
himself, herself, itself	themselves

Unit 2: **A whale of a time!**

Let's find them!

Underline all the **personal**, **possessive** and **reflexive pronouns** in the text, and then choose eight of them to write in the spaces below. Don't use the ones in bold. Use the list of pronouns in the table to help you find the words in the text.

1. _____
2. _____
3. _____
4. _____
5. _____
6. _____
7. _____
8. _____

Let's go to the next step!

Replace the underlined words with a **pronoun**.
For example: The whales were migrating to <u>the whales'</u> breeding ground. _their_

1. Mr Smith left <u>Mr Smith's</u> camera on the boat. _____
2. Whales are mammals because <u>whales</u> give birth to live young. _____
3. Susan and Jane showed <u>Alex and Sam</u> the photos of the whales. _____
4. <u>The tour guide</u> let us use his camera to take photos of the whales. _____
5. Mrs Robertson said that the book about whales was <u>Mrs Robertson's</u>. _____
6. The humpback whale blew air out of <u>the humpback whale's</u> blowhole. _____
7. The little girl clapped <u>the little girl's</u> hands when <u>the little girl</u> saw the whale. _____

Let's aim high now!

Tip! Reminder! Reflexive pronouns end in *self* or *selves*.

Complete each of these sentences with a **reflexive pronoun**.
For example: We wanted to see the whales for <u>ourselves</u>.

1. I hurt _____ when I slipped on the boat.
2. "You can see for _____ how big the whale is," said Dad.
3. The whale arched its back as it lifted _____ out of the water.
4. The whales seemed to be enjoying _____ in the water.
5. We wore wide-brimmed hats to protect _____ from the sun.
6. She wanted a photo of _____ with the whale in the background.
7. The little boy hauled _____ onto the bench to get a better view of the whales.

Saving the whale

"**What is that**?" asked little Myrna, pointing to a large, dark object on the beach.

"It must be **something** the tide washed in during the night," said James. "Who wants to go down and investigate?"

Before Myrna or Ben could answer, they saw someone rushing towards the object with a sense of urgency. He was followed by others, each carrying buckets.

"What are those for, James?" asked Myrna.

But James didn't answer. He had gone to his room to get his shoes. "Come on," he said. "This is an emergency. A whale has stranded itself."

It seemed that everyone in the village wanted to help save the beached whale. They vowed they would do everything they could to keep the animal alive until the tide came in and they could coax it back into the water.

by Su-Min

This is part of a **narrative**. A narrative tells a story. Su-Min uses **interrogative pronouns** to ask questions, **demonstrative pronouns** to point out specific people and things, and **indefinite pronouns** to refer to people and things in a general way while telling a story about a beached whale.

Interrogative pronouns ask questions; for example, **What is that?**
The other interrogative pronouns are Who?, Whom?, Whose? and Which?

Demonstrative pronouns point out specific people or things; for example, **that** points out the object on the beach.
The other demonstrative pronouns are *this*, *these* and *those*.

Indefinite pronouns refer to people and things in a general way; for example, **something** refers to whatever it is the tide washed in during the night.

Let's find them!

Tip!

Here are some **indefinite pronouns**: all, another, any, anyone, anybody, both, each, either, everyone, everybody, everything, no-one, none, nothing, others, some, someone, something, somebody and whatever.

Underline all the **interrogative**, **demonstrative** and **indefinite pronouns** in the text and then choose eight of them to write in the spaces. Don't use the ones in bold.

 1 _____

 2 _____

Unit 2: A whale of a time!

3 _____   6 _____
4 _____   7 _____
5 _____   8 _____

Let's go to the next step!

Complete each sentence with an **interrogative** or **demonstrative pronoun**.
For example: That is the biggest whale I have ever seen!

1. _____ whale calf is very playful.
2. Those whales are bigger than _____ .
3. "_____ is my first whale watching trip," she said.
4. "_____ is the biggest whale in the world?" he asked.
5. "_____ camera is this?" asked the captain of the boat.
6. "_____ have you done with my book on whales?" asked Dad.
7. "_____ wants to come with me on a whale watching expedition?" I asked.

Let's aim high now!

Complete each sentence with an **indefinite pronoun** from the box.
Use each word once.

| everything | something | someone | any | both | no-one | none | anyone |

1. _____ cried, "There's a whale!"
2. We were looking for whales, but didn't see _____ .
3. That man seems to know _____ about whales.
4. We scanned the ocean for whales, but saw _____ .
5. We asked if _____ had seen a whale, but _____ had.
6. The children spotted _____ that looked like a whale on the beach.
7. We knew there were two whales when _____ leaped out of the water.

10   Year 6 Grammar and Punctuation Workbook

Let's put it together now!

Su-Min is unsure where to put these **pronouns** in this section of her narrative. Help her fill them in correctly.

| mine | itself | whose | she | you | somebody | this |

"_____ bucket is _____?" asked one of the village boys.

"It's _____," replied Myrna, "but _____ can use it."

Myrna was exhausted. _____ watched as people tried to coax the whale back into the water. She asked _____ why it had beached _____, but he couldn't give her an answer.

Let's have fun!

Draw lines to match the **pronouns** on the fish to these parts of the whale's body:

the personal pronouns to its stomach
the possessive pronouns to its back
the reflexive pronouns to its tail

the interrogative pronouns to its large fin
the demonstrative pronouns to its jaw
the indefinite pronouns above its blowhole.

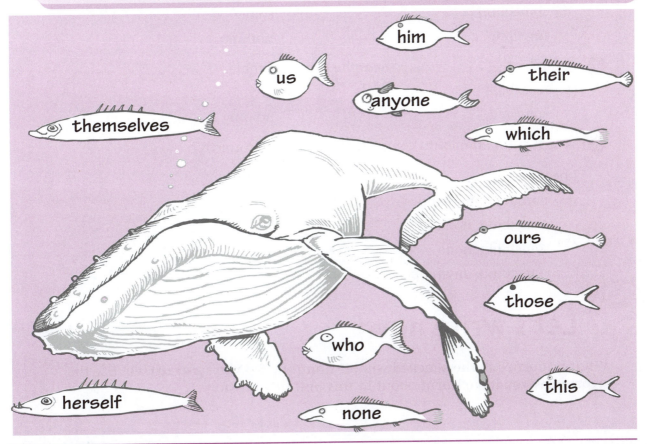

Unit 2: **A whale of a time!**

Let's have a test!

In questions 1–7, which pronoun completes the sentence correctly?

1 _____ showed us their photos of whales.
- ○ Them
- ○ They
- ○ Him
- ○ Her

2 We checked _____ tickets before we boarded the boat.
- ○ ours
- ○ us
- ○ yours
- ○ our

3 The children entertained _____ by looking for whales.
- ○ themselves
- ○ ourselves
- ○ yourselves
- ○ myself

4 "_____ knows what a humpback whale looks like?" he asked.
- ○ What
- ○ Whose
- ○ Who
- ○ Which

5 "I also have _____," he said, showing me a whale's tooth.
- ○ that
- ○ this
- ○ these
- ○ those

6 We listened for whale sounds, but heard _____.
- ○ something
- ○ anything
- ○ some
- ○ nothing

7 I didn't see _____ near the beached whale.
- ○ somebody
- ○ someone
- ○ anyone
- ○ no-one

8 Which pair of pronouns completes this sentence correctly?

I heard _____ in the water, but didn't see _____.
- ○ nothing, something
- ○ something, nothing
- ○ something, none
- ○ something, anything

Let's write now!

What happened to the beached whale? Continue Su-Min's **narrative**. Use the **pronouns** you have learnt about in this unit in your story.

Unit 3 Chocolate

Focus Adjectives

A bitter-sweet story

People have been eating chocolate for centuries. However, it hasn't always been the smooth, sweet substance we know today.

Chocolate comes from the cacao plant, which is native to South and Central America. When the Spanish conquered the region in the sixteenth century, the **local** people had already worked out how to turn the dark brown beans from the plant into a **bitter** drink that they called *chocolatl*. The Spaniards added sugar cane to it to make it sweeter and they took this new drink back to Europe with them. But it was another **three hundred** years before someone found a way of making chocolate that could be eaten. After improving its taste and consistency by adding newly discovered spices and squeezing some of the cocoa butter out of the beans, an **English** company finally developed the **first** edible chocolate in the nineteenth century.

by Julia

This is a **factual recount**. A factual recount retells events in the order in which they happened. Julia uses different types of **adjectives** (describing words) to give more information about nouns in her recount of the history of chocolate.

Adjectives are describing words. They give more information about nouns; for example, **local** gives us more information about the noun *people*.

Types of adjectives include
- describing adjectives; for example, **bitter**.
- numbering adjectives; for example, **three hundred**.
- proper adjectives (formed from proper nouns); for example, **English**.
- ordering adjectives; for example, **first**.

Let's find them!

Find the **adjectives** in the text that give more information about the nouns below. Don't use the ones in bold.

1. substance _____
2. plant _____
3. century _____
4. beans _____
5. drink _____
6. spices _____
7. butter _____
8. chocolate _____

Unit 3: **Chocolate**   13

Let's go to the next step!

Tip!
Antonyms are words that are opposite in meaning; for example, **happy** is the opposite of **sad**.

The **adjectives** in these boxes could be used to describe chocolate. The adjectives in Box B are opposite in meaning to those in Box A. Find the pairs of antonyms and write them in the spaces; for example, ___bitter___ ___sweet___

Box A	Box B
bitter liquid dark expensive	processed traditional sweet
coarse natural patterned	stale unhealthy solid round
hard fresh curly hot flat	boring light smooth soft
nutritious interesting modern	cheap plain straight cold

Let's aim high now!

Tip!
Remember: **suffixes** are endings that are added to words to make new words.

Add a suffix from the box to each noun in brackets to turn it into an **adjective**; for example, **universe → universal**. You might need to change the spelling of the base word, such as dropping the final *e*, before adding the suffix. Use a dictionary to make sure that you spell the words correctly.

| ish | less | ly | al | ic | ful | ous |

1. I chose a chocolate from the (colour) _____ box.
2. That shop is (fame) _____ for its chocolate statues.
3. Eating chocolate is a (magic) _____ experience.
4. The (friend) _____ girl gave me one of her chocolates.
5. Only a (fool) _____ person would eat all that chocolate!
6. We shared our chocolate with a (home) _____ man.
7. This is a very (base) _____ recipe for chocolate cake.

The health benefits of chocolate

When it comes to tasty treats, there's nothing **tastier** than chocolate. Opinion polls show that it's one of the most popular foods in the world. And now we can eat it without feeling guilty!

According to the **latest** research, the cocoa in chocolate contains flavonoids that are good for our health. The down side is that it is the darker varieties—the bitter ones—that are the healthiest. These are **less popular** than the lighter, sweeter varieties, which are not as healthy.

One of the **most interesting** things that scientists have discovered about chocolate is that it can turn us into happier, smarter people! They warn, however, that most chocolate contains lots of sugar, so we shouldn't eat too much of it.

This is an **article** from a magazine. One of the purposes of a magazine article is to inform. The author uses **adjectives** to compare people and things with each other while telling about the health benefits of chocolate.

Rule!

Adjectives can compare people, places and things with each other; for example, **tastier** compares chocolate with other tasty treats.
- If two people, places or things are being compared, the adjective usually ends in *er*; for example, **tast**ier. These are called **comparative adjectives**.
- If more than two people, animals, places or things are being compared, the adjective usually ends in *est*; for example, **lat**est. These are called **superlative adjectives.**

When an adjective consists of more than two syllables, we use the words
- **more** or **less** in front of it when comparing two people, places or things; for example, **less popular**.
- **most** or **least** in front of it when comparing more than two people, places or things; for example, **most** interesting.

Let's find them!

Tip!

For **adjectives** that end in *y*, change the *y* to *i* before adding *er* or *est*. For example, **tasty** → **tastier, tastiest**. Some **adjectives of degree** don't follow the usual rules. For example, **good, better, best; bad, worse, worst; far, further, furthest; little, less, least; some/many/much, more** and **most**.

Underline the **comparative** and **superlative adjectives** in the text and choose eight of them to write in the spaces.

1. _____
2. _____

Unit 3: Chocolate 15

3 _____
4 _____
5 _____

6 _____
7 _____
8 _____

Let's go to the next step!

Fill in the **comparative** and **superlative** forms of these **adjectives**. The first two lines have been done for you.

Adjective	Comparative	Superlative
smooth	smoother	smoothest
delicious	more delicious	most delicious
crunchy		
creamy		
expensive		
good		
rich		
soft		
fancy		
fresh		
scrumptious		
pretty		

Let's aim high now!

Complete these sentences by using the correct form of the **adjective** in brackets.

1. This bar of chocolate is (crispy) _____ than that one.
2. That is the (large) _____ chocolate bar I have ever seen!
3. That is the (bad) _____ chocolate brand in the world!
4. We all had some chocolate, but Jamie ate the (much) _____.
5. Vera's chocolate cake has a (good) _____ texture than mine.
6. I chose the (colourful) _____ of the two boxes of chocolates.
7. Last night Mum made the (wonderful) _____ chocolate dessert I've ever tasted!

Let's put it together now!

This student has written eight **adjectives** incorrectly in her recount about the world's biggest chocolate bar. Underline the mistakes and write the corrections in the spaces below.

In 2011, a chocolate factory in England celebrated its 100th birthday in a very tastier way: it created the world's larger chocolate bar. The bar, which weighed 5827 kg, was almost 300 kg heavy than the previous record. The fifty people who worked on the project spent many longer hours carrying the mixture in buckets to the enormous mould. They said it was the bigger, tiring, but also the enjoyable challenge they had ever faced at the factory. Afterwards, the hugest bar was broken up and sold to raise money for charity.

Let's have fun!

Find the correct path down this slab to win the box of chocolates at the bottom!

Start by colouring in the block that contains the **superlative adjective** in the top row, and then colour all the other superlative adjectives by moving either downwards or sideways.

fewer	best	brown	gentler	fuller
most attractive	most powerful	narrower	flaky	warmer
least / chunkiest	crooked	calm	messy	fluffier / delightful
most colourful	foamiest	tastiest	hungrier	emptier / amused
flatter	healthier	fastest	loveliest	most beautiful

Unit 3: **Chocolate**

Let's have a test!

1 Which sentence contains an adjective?
- ○ I love chocolate!
- ○ I have already eaten the chocolate.
- ○ I bought the chocolates yesterday.
- ○ Chocolate is a delicious treat.

2 Which sentence does **not** contain an adjective?
- ○ Dark chocolate is good for you.
- ○ I put the chocolate in the fridge.
- ○ The chocolates were expensive.
- ○ They put colourful wrappers around the chocolates.

3 Which adjective completes this sentence correctly?

I put a _____ raisins in the chocolate sauce.
- ○ some
- ○ few
- ○ one
- ○ much

4 Which adjective does **not** complete this sentence correctly?

There are _____ chocolates in the box.
- ○ assorted
- ○ several
- ○ any
- ○ many

In questions 5–8, which option completes the sentence correctly?

5 Some chocolates are _____ than others.
- ○ healthy
- ○ healthyer
- ○ healthier
- ○ healthiest

6 That is the _____ I've ever travelled to buy chocolates!
- ○ furtherest
- ○ furtherer
- ○ furthest
- ○ further

7 He won the prize for the _____ of all the chocolate statues.
- ○ more hilarious
- ○ hilarious
- ○ hilariouser
- ○ most hilarious

8 Some varieties of chocolate are _____ than others.
- ○ popular
- ○ less popular
- ○ least popular
- ○ most popular

Let's write now!

Write an **article** for your school newsletter entitled 'The delights of chocolate!' Find information for your article by looking in books or on the Internet. Make sure you use **adjectives** to describe and compare people and things in your article.

Unit 4: Shipwrecks

Focus: Verbs; verb groups

The sinking of the *Titanic*

The *Titanic* set sail from Southampton on April 10th 1912. Four days later it **hit** an iceberg and sank. Of the 2200 people on board, only 700 survived.

Although this event happened more than one hundred years ago, people **are** still fascinated by it. One of the reasons for this is that the *Titanic* was the biggest, most luxurious ship of its time. In fact, people **had** the idea that it was unsinkable! Also, the telegraph and telephone had recently been invented. This meant that news of the disaster spread quickly and it was immediately reported in newspapers around the world.

The wreck of the *Titanic* was discovered in 1985. It **lies** 4000 m below the surface of the Atlantic Ocean, about 700 km west of New York. Although there **has been** talk of raising it, many people believe that this **will never happen**.

This is an **article** from a **website**. One of the purposes of a website is to share information, ideas and opinions. The author uses different types of **verbs** to tell us what is happening and when it happens while sharing information and opinions on the sinking of the *Titanic*.

Verbs are the most important words in sentences. Without them, sentences don't make sense.

Verbs tell us what is happening. They can be
- doing words; for example, **hit**.
- being words; for example, **are**.
- having words; for example, **had**.

Verbs also tell us when something happens.
- The **present tense** tells us that something is happening now; for example, It **lies** 4000 m below the surface.
- The **past tense** tells us that something has already happened; for example, there **has been** talk of raising it.
- The **future tense** tells us that something has yet to happen; for example, this **will never happen**.

Rule!

Rules for writing past tense verbs
- Most **past tense verbs** are formed by adding *d* or *ed* to the present form; for example, **happened**.
- Some verbs change their spelling or pronunciation in the past tense; for example, **sank**.
- The verbs **be**, **being**, **am**, **is** and **are** change to **been**, **was** and **were** in the past tense.
- The verbs **have** and **has** change to **had** in the past tense.

Rule for writing future tense verbs
- **Future tense** verbs are formed by writing **will** or **am/are/is going to** before the present tense verb; for example, This <u>will</u> never happen.

Unit 4: Shipwrecks 19

Let's find them!

Find these **verbs** in the text and write down whether they are in the **present** or **past tense**.

1. set sail _____
2. survived _____
3. is _____
4. was _____
5. meant _____
6. reported _____
7. spread _____
8. lies _____

Let's go to the next step!

Underline the **verb** in brackets that completes each sentence correctly.

1. I (lend/lent) him my diving gear yesterday.
2. The ship (sink/sank) after it hit the iceberg.
3. They will (explore/explored) the wrecked ship.
4. Parts of the wreck will (float/floated) to the surface.
5. He said he (wanted/want) to go with us to explore the wreck.
6. The sinking of the *Titanic* (makes/made) headline news at the time.
7. (Remind/Reminded) me to watch the documentary about the *Titanic*.

Let's aim high now!

Underline the **verbs** in these sentences and then rewrite each one in the **past tense**.

For example: They <u>will find</u> the wreck. _____ found _____

> **Tip!**
> Some sentences contain more than one **verb**!

1. He sees many shipwrecks. _____
2. She writes about the *Titanic*. _____
3. I think the shipwreck is over there. _____
4. Lots of people climb into the lifeboat. _____
5. People freeze to death in the icy water. _____
6. I have an interesting book about shipwrecks. _____
7. They explore the wrecks when they go to the island. _____

From: Olio610
Subject: Hello Gramps
Date: 15 January
To: Robert Carter robjcart@eagle.com.au

Hi Gramps

We **are having** a great time in Western Australia. We visited the Shipwreck Galleries in Fremantle and saw part of the hull and other items from the wreck of the *Batavia*. Remember you once told me about that. Well now I can tell you a bit more! The ship was wrecked in 1629, 80 km off the coast of WA near Beacon Island. And now for the gruesome part! While the ship's commander and other officers went off **to find** help, one of the crew members and his followers murdered 125 of the 268 people left behind. He was also planning to steal the ship's treasure. But when help finally arrived, he and his followers were arrested and either hanged or imprisoned. I'll tell you the rest when we get home.

I hope you're not missing us too much, Gramps. We should be home next week. Don't forget to feed my fish.

Lots of love, Olivia

This is an **email**. An email is a way of communicating with others. Olivia uses different **verb groups** to tell Gramps what happened when the *Batavia* was wrecked.

A **verb group** is a group of words that is built around a verb.

Most verb groups are formed when one or more auxiliary or helping verbs is placed before the main verb; for example, **are having**.

The **auxiliary verbs** are:
am, are, be, been, can, could, did, do, does, had, has, have, is, may, might, must, shall, should, was, were, will, would.

Verb groups are also formed by placing *to* before a verb; for example, **to find**. (This is known as an **infinitive**.)

Let's find them!

Find these **verb groups** in the text.
The verb group that is built around the verb

 tell _____

 Tip!

A common mistake is to write '**could of**' and '**would of**' instead of **could have** and **would have**. Be careful not to make this mistake!

Unit 4: **Shipwrecks**

2. wrecked _____
3. planning _____
4. steal _____

5. arrested _____
6. be _____
7. forget _____

Let's go to the next step!

Underline the **verb groups** in these sentences.
For example: I <u>am planning to visit</u> the shipwreck soon.

1. The divers were hoping to find the shipwreck.
2. They had to abandon the search for the wreck.
3. The octopus had made its home in the shipwreck.
4. They have found a chest of old coins in the wreck.
5. They are going to explore the old shipwreck tomorrow.
6. We are going to watch a documentary about the *Titanic*.
7. I could make out the shape of a hull through my goggles.

Let's aim high now!

Complete the **verb groups** in these sentences with one of these **auxiliary verbs**. Use each word once only.

have	did	will	would	should	was	had	is

1. The old ship _____ lying at the bottom of the ocean.
2. "We _____ have to search elsewhere," said the diver.
3. The boy _____ looking at a picture of an old shipwreck.
4. The divers _____ searched everywhere for the wreck.
5. They _____ not think they _____ ever find the wreck.
6. "I _____ never seen so much treasure!" exclaimed the diver.
7. "We _____ find the wreck soon," said the leader of the expedition.

22   **Year 6 Grammar and Punctuation Workbook**

Let's put it together now!

This student has written six **verbs** incorrectly in his **article** about the *Andrea Doria*. Underline the mistakes and write the corrections in the spaces below.

In 1956 the Italian ship, the *Andrea Doria*, collide with another ship while on its way to New York. Although there was enough lifeboats on board, half of them couldn't been used because of the way the ship were listing. Luckily the ship stay afloat for eleven hours, which gave rescuers plenty of time to get to the vessel. These days, divers liked to look for treasure in and around the wreck of the *Andrea Doria*.

_____   _____
_____   _____
_____   _____

Let's have fun!

Fit the following **verbs** into the blocks going down and the names of the famous shipwrecks into the blocks going across. The number of blocks and the letter in each cross are your clues.

Shipwrecks: Victory Sultana Estonia Vasa Carpathia Rhone Vampire
Verbs: discover survive wrecked explore drowned rescue sailed

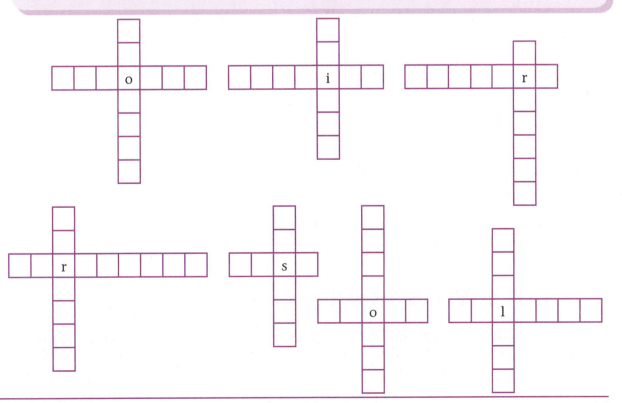

Unit 4: **Shipwrecks**

Let's have a test!

In questions 1–3, which word(s) completes the sentence correctly?

1 The wreck _____ in deep water.
- ○ are
- ○ am
- ○ were
- ○ is

2 These days the diver often _____ old wrecks.
- ○ find
- ○ finding
- ○ finds
- ○ found

3 Next year we _____ to Western Australia to see the Shipwreck Galleries.
- ○ are going
- ○ went
- ○ will going
- ○ goes

4 Which sentence has been written **incorrectly**?
- ○ There is a shipwreck near the reef.
- ○ He sometimes seen the wreck.
- ○ Sam likes to dive there.
- ○ He is going to explore it today.

In questions 5–6, which word completes the sentence correctly?

5 The diver has _____ to put on his flippers.
- ○ forget
- ○ forgot
- ○ forgets
- ○ forgotten

6 The divers were _____ to find the wreck.
- ○ try
- ○ trying
- ○ tried
- ○ tries

In questions 7–8, which word does **not** complete the sentence correctly?

7 The diver thinks she _____ find the wreck this time.
- ○ might
- ○ can
- ○ will
- ○ does

8 The ship _____ there for a long time.
- ○ has been
- ○ have been
- ○ will be
- ○ could be

Let's write now!

Look in books or on the Internet for information on a famous shipwreck. Write an **article** about it for a website your class is creating. Use different types of **verbs** in your article.

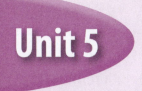

Unit 5 — We're going camping!

Focus: Sentences; subjects and predicates

Unhappy campers (Part 1)

"Guess where we're going," Dad asked at breakfast one morning. **Dad is always full of beans in the morning.**

Mum raised an eyebrow, and gave him that "Well, where is it this time?" look. She was probably remembering the last time Dad said **"Guess where we're going."** We had ended up looking for dinosaur bones in some remote part of the Australian outback.

Chloe, my 14-year-old sister, rolled her eyes. **She was probably thinking the same thing.** She says that since our outback adventure, she hasn't been able to enjoy food like she used to: now everything tastes of red dust! I, on the other hand, had enjoyed looking for dinosaur bones (even though we didn't find any) and the red dust hadn't bothered me in the least. So I asked, "Where are we going, Dad?"

"We're going camping!" Dad announced, beaming from ear to ear.

by Ethan

This is part of a **narrative**. Remember: a narrative tells a story. Ethan uses different types of **sentences** to tell about Dad's announcement at breakfast one morning.

Sentences
- are groups of words that make sense when they stand on their own; for example, **Dad is always full of beans in the morning.**
- always start with a capital letter and end with a full stop, question mark or exclamation mark; for example, **We're going camping!**
- contain at least one verb or verb group; for example, **She <u>was</u> probably <u>thinking</u> the same thing.**
- are usually **statements**. They start with a capital letter and end with a full stop; for example, **Guess where we're going.**

Questions ask for information and end with a question mark; for example, *Are we going camping?*

Exclamations express strong feelings or emotions and end with an exclamation mark; for example, *What an awful campsite!*

Commands give orders. They start with an action verb and end with a full stop or exclamation mark; for example, *<u>Put</u> the tent over there.*

Let's find them!

Underline the verbs and verb groups in these **sentences** based on information in the text.

1. Dad is always full of beans in the morning.
2. Mum raised an eyebrow.
3. Chloe, my 14-year-old sister, rolled her eyes.
4. Since our outback adventure, she hasn't been able to enjoy her food.
5. I had enjoyed looking for dinosaur bones.
6. The red dust hadn't bothered me in the least.
7. "Where are we going, Dad?"

Let's go to the next step!

Fill in the correct **punctuation mark** at the end of each of these **sentences**.

1. I hate sleeping in a tent ◯
2. Park the camper van in that spot ◯
3. Have you ever been camping before ◯
4. Where are we going camping this year ◯
5. We go camping at least once every year ◯
6. Find out how long we can stay at the campsite ◯
7. Tonight we'll toast marshmallows around the campfire ◯

Let's aim high now!

Rewrite each of these **sentences** as a **command**.
For example: You should buy a new tent.   _Buy a new tent._

1. Should you wash your sleeping bag? _____
2. You should keep the campsite clean. _____
3. You must stay away from the campfire. _____
4. Could you help Dad pack away the tent? _____
5. You mustn't be a nuisance to other campers. _____
6. Campers shouldn't make a noise late at night. _____
7. You could find a campsite that is close to the sea. _____

Unhappy campers (Part 2)

"But we went camping when we looked for dinosaur bones," protested Chloe, "and it was awful!"

I felt I had to defend Dad here. We'd stayed in luxury tents and everything had been laid on for us. But before I could say anything, Dad dropped his next bombshell.

"This time we're going to an island!" he announced grandly, as though we'd just won first prize in the lottery.

Mum and Chloe perked up at this. "An island?" Chloe crooned.

"An island!" Dad repeated. "And this time there'll be no running water, no electricity and no TV or mobile phone reception. It'll just be us and the great outdoors."

"No mobile phone reception," squeaked Chloe. "No running water," mumbled Mum.

Looking as pleased as Punch, Dad turned to me. "What do you think, son?" What did I think? I thought I had the best dad in the world. He has such brilliant ideas!

by Ethan

This is another part of the **narrative**. Ethan uses **sentences** with **subjects** and **predicates** to tell about the family's reaction to Dad's announcement.

Most **sentences** consist of two parts:
- the **subject**—the person or thing that the sentence is about.
- the **predicate**—what the sentence is about.

For example: **Mum and Chloe perked up at this.** In this sentence, the subject is *Mum and Chloe* and the predicate is *perked up at this*.

Rule! The **predicate** contains the verb.

Let's find them!

Underline the **subjects** in these sentences based on information in the text.

1. Chloe protested that they went camping last time.
2. I felt I had to defend Dad.
3. That time, we had stayed in luxury tents.
4. Then Dad dropped his next bombshell.
5. Mum couldn't believe the island had no running water!

Tip!
The **subject** does not always come at the beginning of a sentence; for example, Looking as pleased as Punch, <u>Dad</u> turned to me.

Unit 5: **We're going camping!**

6 Dad turned to his son.

7 Dad and the narrator thought it was a brilliant idea.

Let's go to the next step!

> **Tip!**
> Remember: the **subject** of a sentence must agree with the verb in the **predicate**. For example, The campsite <u>is</u> luxurious. The campsites <u>are</u> luxurious.

Make these **subjects** agree with their verbs by underlining the correct option in brackets.

1 (The boy/The boys) stay in the tent at night.

2 The driver (is parking/are parking) the caravan.

3 Those campers (goes/go) to the beach every day.

4 This groundsheet (belongs/belong) to the people in that tent.

5 The people who run the campsite (lives/live) in that big house.

6 After lunch, (Dad/Dad and I) always go for a walk on the beach.

7 At the campsite, (Mum/Mum and Joanne) was preparing dinner.

Let's aim high now!

Match the **subjects** in Column A with their **predicates** in Column B. Shade the matching pairs the same colour.

Column A	Column B
The Australian flag	have swimming pools.
The campsite	have bought a new campervan.
Not all campsites	protects the tents in windy weather.
The row of trees	is fluttering above the campsite.
A family of ducks	was situated a long way from the beach.
Our neighbours	has got a big caravan.
My uncle	was swimming in the pond next to our campsite.

28   Year 6 Grammar and Punctuation Workbook

Let's put it together now!

This student has made some mistakes in this section of her narrative. She has used the wrong **punctuation marks** at the end of some of her **sentences**, and some of her **subjects** don't agree with their verbs. Use a red pen to make the corrections for her.

The children has just arrived at the campsite when the storm started.

"How long do you think this will last!" asked Gabrielle.

"I'm not sure," replied the camp leader. "These storms can go on for a long time?"

He looked at Sammy, who were reading a book. "What is you reading, Sammy." he asked.

Sammy held up the book. "It's by my favourite author," he said. "My friends and I loves his books."

Let's have fun!

The words and **punctuation** in these sentences have become muddled. Unscramble them and write them correctly in the spaces below.

1. been have ? times How camping many you

_____

_____

2. was camping ! How trip that amazing

_____

_____

3. caravan Show is where . us parked your

_____

_____

4. on I . enjoy camping going trips really

_____

_____

5. you at campsite Which ? staying are

_____

_____

Unit 5: **We're going camping!**

Let's have a test!

1 Which sentence has the correct punctuation?
- ○ When are you going camping this year!
- ○ Where are you going camping this year?
- ○ Are you going camping this year.
- ○ We are going camping this year?

2 Which punctuation mark completes this sentence correctly?

That is the tent I would like to buy _____
- ○ !
- ○ .
- ○ ?
- ○ "

3 Which of these sentences is a command?
- ○ Dad bought a new trailer.
- ○ Will you light a campfire?
- ○ Wait in the caravan.
- ○ They are sitting beside our tent.

4 Which word completes this sentence correctly?

_____ to the rain beating against the tent.
- ○ Listen
- ○ Hear
- ○ Watch
- ○ Feel

5 Who or what is the subject of this sentence?

The lady in the caravan has given us some lollies.
- ○ The lady
- ○ caravan
- ○ lollies
- ○ The lady in the caravan

6 Which option completes this sentence correctly?

They _____ on a camping holiday.
- ○ is going
- ○ was going
- ○ has gone
- ○ are going

7 Which pair of words completes this text correctly?

He _____ putting up the tent. _____ he need any help?
- ○ is, Do
- ○ are, Does
- ○ is, Did
- ○ is, Does

8 Which word can be left out of this sentence without changing the meaning?

I thought that he was going to take down the tent.
- ○ that
- ○ was
- ○ down
- ○ the

Let's write now!

Continue writing the **narrative** Unhappy campers. Tell what happens when the family gets to the island. Try to use all the different types of **sentences** in your narrative, and make sure your **subjects** and **verbs** agree!

30   Year 6 Grammar and Punctuation Workbook

Unit 6 — Courage

★ Focus
Verbal adjectives; verbal nouns

Moral courage

Moral courage means doing the right thing, even if the consequences seem frightening. There are many **inspiring stories** of people who have risked their reputations, and even their lives, to stand up for what they believe is right. Doctor Martin Luther King Jr is a shining example of someone who stood up for his beliefs, as are Mahatma Gandhi and Mother Theresa.

Every day we have the opportunity to do the right thing. If someone is in trouble, we can lend a helping hand. If we find a lost wallet or other item of value, we can hand it in. Gossip might be interesting, but we shouldn't be listening to or repeating it. We can all learn important lessons by studying the lives of **celebrated heroes** like Doctor Martin Luther King Jr, whose courage we admire.

This is an **article** from a **website**. Remember: one of the purposes of a website is to share information, ideas and opinions. The author uses **verbal adjectives** to describe nouns while informing us what it means to have moral courage.

Verbal adjectives are verbs that are used as adjectives. Like adjectives, they describe nouns.

Verbal adjectives end in
- *ing*; for example, **inspiring stories**.
- *ed*; for example, **celebrated heroes**.

Let's find them!

Find these words in the text and write down whether they are being used as **verbs** or **adjectives**. Remember: adjectives describe something.

1. frightening _____
2. shining _____

Tip!
Some past tense **verbs** that are used as adjectives are irregular and do not end in *ed*; for example, **broken promises**.

Unit 6: Courage — 31

3. helping _____

4. lost _____

5. interesting _____

6. listening _____

7. repeating _____

Let's go to the next step!

Complete each of these sentences with a **verbal adjective** from the box.

> missing   freezing   punishing   charred   broken   stranded   growing   crumbling   pleased

1. There was _____ concern for the firefighters' safety.

2. All that was left after the fire was bits of _____ wood.

3. Rescuers entered the house through a _____ window.

4. They resumed the search for the _____ hikers at daybreak.

5. The man risked his life when he entered the _____ building.

6. We were _____ to hear that he had completed the _____ race.

7. Rescuers braved the _____ conditions to save the _____ skiers.

Let's aim high now!

Complete these sentences by changing the **verb** in brackets to an **adjective**.
For example: The girl saved the (injure) <u>injured</u> animal.

1. The kind boy comforted the (cry) _____ child.

2. The rescue team reached the (scare) _____ children.

3. Helping others can be a (reward) _____ experience.

4. They faced the (terrify) _____ ordeal with great courage.

5. She admitted her wrongdoing in a (write) _____ apology.

6. He carried on running, even though he was (exhaust) _____.

7. It was his (fight) _____ spirit that got him through the difficult times.

Physical courage

Physical courage is when we push our bodies to the limit to protect ourselves or someone else, or to achieve an ambition. **Climbing a high mountain** is an example of physical courage. So is defending yourself or others against an enemy, or sailing around the world in a small yacht. Training for a marathon or jumping into the water to save someone from being drowned are further examples of physical courage.

We have all displayed physical courage at some point in our lives. Skills that we may take for granted now, like walking, swimming and riding a bike, were once challenges that we had to overcome. In that sense, we are all heroes!

*This is another **article** from a **website**. The author uses **verbal nouns** to name actions while informing us what it means to have physical courage.*

Verbal nouns
- are verbs that do the work of nouns.
- name actions.
- end in *ing*; for example, **Climbing a high mountain**.

Let's find them!

Underline all the **verbal nouns** in the text and then write seven of them in the spaces. Don't use the one in bold.

1. _____
2. _____
3. _____

Unit 6: Courage

4 _____   6 _____
5 _____   7 _____

Let's go to the next step!

Underline the **verbal nouns** in these sentences.
For example: <u>Exercising</u> requires commitment.

1. Bullying is not something to be proud of.
2. Hurdling requires a lot of skill and training.
3. Supporting good causes is one of his hobbies!
4. Diving to great depths requires great courage.
5. Overcoming obstacles can make you stronger.
6. Reporting bad behaviour sometimes takes courage.
7. Protecting the environment is very important to him

Let's aim high now!

Which activities do you associate with these people? Complete each sentence with a **verbal noun** from the box.

| flying | debating | caring | cycling | treating | sprinting | coaching |

1. A nurse's job involves _____ for others.
2. A vet's job involves _____ sick animals.
3. The pilot took up _____ when he was quite old.
4. The athlete took up _____ on the advice of his coaches.
5. The politician took part in _____ when he was at school.
6. The basketball player took up _____ after he got injured.
7. The winner of the Tour de France took up _____ when he was very young.

Let's put it together now!

This student is unsure where the following words belong in his sentence about people who do courageous things. Help him fill in the words.

| war-torn | burning | working | rushing | orphaned | trapped | starving |

People who perform acts of bravery, like _____ into _____ buildings to save those _____ inside, or _____ to help _____ or _____ children in _____ countries, are true heroes who deserve our respect.

Let's have fun!

These **verbal adjectives** and **verbal nouns** are hiding in the wordsearch puzzle. Can you find them? The words go forwards, backwards, up and down.

| volunteering | mountaineering | trying | learning | rescued | completed | burnt | injured |

x	l	t	v	o	l	u	n	t	e	e	r	i	n	g
c	e	x	v	w	q	h	y	r	e	s	c	u	e	d
t	a	b	a	s	s	d	j	f	n	d	z	n	f	d
n	r	j	h	g	n	e	y	l	f	e	r	g	j	k
r	n	r	w	c	n	r	f	h	j	y	z	n	m	o
u	i	q	v	a	q	u	h	j	d	s	h	i	i	k
b	n	t	i	h	g	j	h	s	h	e	g	y	g	d
a	g	j	n	n	z	n	n	v	s	n	w	r	r	t
g	n	i	h	c	t	i	w	h	h	i	k	t	c	x
a	g	n	i	r	e	e	n	i	a	t	n	u	o	m
z	y	d	e	t	e	l	p	m	o	c	u	h	d	a

Unit 6: **Courage**   35

Let's have a test!

In questions 1–6, which word completes the sentence correctly?

1. We faced a _____ task.
   - ○ challenge
   - ○ challenging
   - ○ challenged
   - ○ challenger

2. The _____ crowd watched him land safely.
   - ○ relieve
   - ○ relieving
   - ○ relieved
   - ○ relief

3. I found his behaviour very _____.
   - ○ threatening
   - ○ threatened
   - ○ threat
   - ○ threatens

4. The _____ boy apologised for his aggressive behaviour.
   - ○ embarrass
   - ○ embarrassing
   - ○ embarrasses
   - ○ embarrassed

5. _____ in yourself is important.
   - ○ Believe
   - ○ Believed
   - ○ Believing
   - ○ Believes

6. I told him that _____ wouldn't get the job done.
   - ○ complain
   - ○ complaint
   - ○ complained
   - ○ complaining

In questions 7–8, which sequence of words completes the sentence correctly?

7. _____ on _____ well requires discipline.
   - ○ Focusing, doing
   - ○ Focused, doing
   - ○ Doing, focusing
   - ○ Focusing, do

8. _____ about _____ is not enough.
   - ○ Dreamed, success
   - ○ Dreaming, succeed
   - ○ Dreaming, succeeding
   - ○ Dreaming, succeeded

Let's write now!

Write an **article** for a website describing what you think it means to have courage. Use **verbal adjectives** and **verbal nouns** in your article.

Unit 7 — Greek mythology

Focus: Adverbs

Theseus and the minotaur

King Minos of Crete was a powerful ruler who treated his subjects **harshly**. He kept a Minotaur—a fearsome creature with a huge appetite—in a labyrinth. Anyone who displeased the king was shut in the labyrinth, where the Minotaur soon devoured them.

Theseus, the prince of Athens, was troubled by what King Minos was doing to his people. He sailed to Crete and, just as he had hoped, was **immediately** thrown into the labyrinth. Fearing that he might become lost in the dark maze, Theseus had carefully hidden a ball of string in his tunic. Now he used it to mark his trail through the labyrinth.

Theseus didn't have long to wait before the Minotaur found him. The young prince fought bravely and killed the monster. He **easily** found his way **out** of the labyrinth and sailed back to Athens under cover of darkness, knowing that Crete would **never** fear the Minotaur again.

by Louise

This is a **myth**. A myth is a traditional story from ancient times. Louise uses **adverbs** to add information about verbs in this myth about Theseus and the Minotaur.

Adverbs give more information about verbs; for example, **harshly** gives more information about how King Minos treated his subjects.

Adverbs tell us
- how something happens or is done; for example, **harshly** (manner). They include words like *gracefully, quickly, awkwardly, badly* and *loudly*.
- when something happens; for example, **immediately** (time). They include words like *early, lately, then, yesterday* and *tomorrow*.
- where something happens; for example, **out** (place). They include words like *near, here, there, up* and *away*.
- how often something happens; for example, **never** (frequency). They include words like *always, occasionally, sometimes, seldom* and *rarely*.
- to what extent something happens; for example, **easily** (degree). They include words like *just, hardly, nearly, fairly* and *almost*.

Let's find them!

Find these **adverbs** in the text and write down which verb or verb group they give more information about. The first one has been done for you.

1. soon _____*devoured*_____

2. just _____
3. immediately _____
4. carefully _____

5. Now _____
6. bravely _____
7. easily _____

Let's go to the next step!

Complete each sentence with an **adverb** from the box. Use each adverb once.

| always | inside | hesitantly | fortunately | instantly | occasionally | angrily |

1. Theseus stepped _____ into the labyrinth.
2. It is _____ entertaining to listen to Greek myths.
3. _____, Theseus managed to kill the Minotaur.
4. The Minotaur roared _____ when Theseus attacked it.
5. Theseus knew _____ that the Minotaur had seen him.
6. Our teacher _____ reads us a story from her book of myths.
7. When King Minos looked _____, he knew that Theseus had escaped.

Let's aim high now!

Underline the **adverbs** in these sentences and write down which type of adverb it is: time, place, manner, frequency or degree.

For example: I have <u>almost</u> finished reading the story of the Minotaur. _degree_

1. I couldn't find the book of myths anywhere. _____
2. He says he will read the other myth tonight. _____
3. Theseus sailed for Crete early in the morning. _____
4. The Minotaur approached Theseus menacingly. _____
5. I often watch a TV program about ancient Greece. _____
6. Theseus' father waited anxiously for his son to return. _____
7. We haven't quite finished the section on Greek mythology. _____

Medusa and Athena

Medusa was an **extremely beautiful** young Athenian girl. However, she boasted **almost continually** about her beauty, claiming that her eyes sparkled **more brightly** than the other girls', her skin glowed more radiantly and her hair shone more lustrously. While visiting the temple one day, she even boasted that she was more beautiful than the goddess, Athena!

Athena was very angry when she heard this and she decided to teach Medusa a lesson. She told her that there were many girls in Athens who worked harder and treated others more kindly, and who were therefore more beautiful than Medusa. As punishment for her vanity, Athena turned Medusa's face into that of a hideous monster, and her beautiful locks into hissing snakes.

by Ahmed

> This is another **myth**. Ahmed uses **adverbs** to add meaning to adjectives and other adverbs and to compare the way in which actions are performed in this myth about Medusa and Athena.

Adverbs can also be used to add meaning to adjectives and other adverbs; for example:
- **extremely** adds meaning to the adjective **beautiful**.
- **almost** adds meaning to the adverb **continually**.

Rule! Like adjectives, **adverbs** have comparative and superlative forms to show degree; for example, sparkled <u>more brightly</u>.

Let's find them!

Find one **adverb** that intensifies or modifies the meaning of an adjective and four adverbs that compare in the text. Write them in the spaces. Don't use the ones in bold.

> **Tip!**
> While some comparative and superlative adverbs take *er* and *est*, most have the words **more**, **most**, **less** or **least** in front of them; for example, **more brightly**.

1. _____
2. _____
3. _____

Unit 7: Greek mythology

4 _____
5 _____

Let's go to the next step!

Underline the **adverb** in brackets that completes each sentence correctly.
For example: Athena gave Medusa (just/also) three days to leave Athens.

1. Medusa was an (fairly/incredibly) beautiful young girl.
2. Medusa was (absolutely/too) beautiful for her own good.
3. She was (so/really) ugly that no one wanted to look at her.
4. She lived an (quite/extremely) lonely life on a distant island.
5. In Greek mythology, Athena was a (entirely/very) powerful goddess.
6. Some people thought that Athena treated Medusa (rather/only) cruelly.
7. Medusa was not (somewhat/overly) concerned when other people warned her of what might happen.

Let's aim high now!

Fill in the missing **adverbs** in this table.

Adverb	Comparative	Superlative
	harder	
early		
		most easily
high		
carefully		
		most comfortably
		soonest
	more often	
	later	
	more enthusiastically	
		furthest
	more curiously	
		fastest
efficiently		

40　　　　　　　　　　　　　　　　　Year 6 Grammar and Punctuation Workbook

Let's put it together now!

This student is unsure where to use these **adverbs** in her retelling of the story of Daedalus and Icarus. Help her to fill them in correctly.

finally	too	more enthusiastically
often	higher	immediately
	very	

King Minos had imprisoned the inventor, Daedalus, and his son, Icarus, in a _____ high tower next to the labyrinth. Birds _____ perched on the window ledge, and when Daedalus noticed some feathers drifting into the tower, he _____ thought of a way of escaping. He told Icarus to collect the feathers. Meanwhile, he worked _____ than he had ever worked before fashioning a pair of wings for himself and his son. He used the wax from their candles to hold the feathers together. When the wings were _____ ready, father and son strapped them on. Daedalus warned his son that the _____ he flew, the more dangerous it would be. Daedalus did not heed his father's warning and flew _____ close to the sun. The wax on his wings melted and he plunged into the sea.

Let's have fun!

Complete the **adverbs** in these sentences by picking letters from the urn. Altogether there are thirty letters in the urn—one for each space. Each time you use a letter, cross it off. There shouldn't be any letters left by the time you have filled in all the spaces.

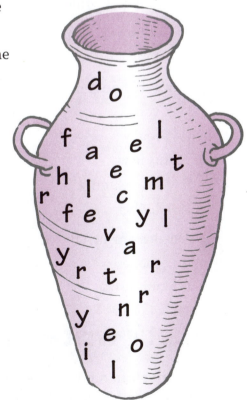

1. Medusa screamed l _ u _ _ y when she heard the snakes hissing.

2. Icarus o _ t _ n got bored in the tower.

3. Boasting about her beauty was a r a _ _ _ _ r silly thing to do.

4. King Minos treated his subjects _ o r e _ r u _ l _ _ _ than the other kings treated their subjects.

5. Theseus left Athens e _ _ l _ in the morning.

6. The goddess Athena was i _ c _ _ _ d _ b _ y beautiful.

7. Daedalus checked the wings m _ s _ c _ _ e _ u _ l _.

8. Daedalus was _ e _ y concerned about his son.

Unit 7: Greek mythology

41

Let's have a test!

1 Which sentence tells how often the action is done?
- ○ Theseus happily tried to help his people.
- ○ Theseus always tried to help his people.
- ○ Theseus tried to help his people then.
- ○ Theseus definitely helped his people.

2 Which sentence tells when the action is done?
- ○ Theseus had seen the Minotaur before.
- ○ Theseus had often seen the Minotaur.
- ○ Theseus had seen the Minotaur somewhere.
- ○ Theseus fought courageously against the Minotaur.

3 Which sentence tells where the action is done?
- ○ Medusa occasionally visited Athena's temple.
- ○ Athena approached Medusa then.
- ○ Athena approached Medusa angrily.
- ○ Athena was standing nearby.

4 Which sentence tells how the action is done?
- ○ Icarus seldom obeyed his father.
- ○ Icarus acted recklessly.
- ○ Icarus took off immediately.
- ○ Icarus flew away from his father.

In questions 5–8, which option completes the sentence correctly?

5 Daedalus was hoping to finish the wings _____ soon.
- ○ too
- ○ quite
- ○ absolutely
- ○ almost

6 Icarus did an _____ silly thing.
- ○ very
- ○ really
- ○ fairly
- ○ extremely

7 Icarus flew _____ than he should have.
- ○ more highly
- ○ higher
- ○ highest
- ○ most highly

8 Daedus finished the wings _____ than expected.
- ○ soonest
- ○ most soon
- ○ more soon
- ○ sooner

Let's write now!

Find a **myth** in a book or on the Internet and rewrite it in your own words. Use as many different types of **adverbs** as possible in your story.

Unit 8 — Chew on this!

★ Focus

Conjunctions; prepositions

Why teeth are important

Eating is something we all have to do to stay alive, but it is also high on most people's list of favourite things to do.

We need healthy teeth to get the most out of our food; however, many of us don't look after our teeth as well as we should. Some food always gets stuck in our teeth when we eat. It then mixes with **saliva and bacteria** to form plaque. If we don't get rid of the plaque, it starts eating through our teeth and we end up with cavities. There are some simple things we can do to prevent cavities from forming.

First, we should brush our teeth for two minutes twice a day. It is also a good idea to brush our teeth after we have eaten fruit or drunk fruit juice or a fizzy drink. This gets rid of acid on the teeth, another cause of tooth decay. Finally, we should cut down on foods containing sugar and starch, such as lollies, biscuits and cake. These foods are harder to remove from our teeth because they are sticky.

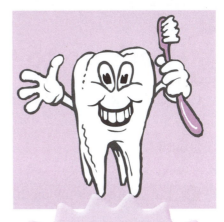

This is an **information leaflet**. Two of the purposes of an information leaflet are to inform and to advise. The author uses **conjunctions** to join sentences and to join words and ideas in sentences while informing us about the causes of cavities and giving advice on how to prevent them from forming.

Conjunctions are joining words. They join
- two sentences to make a single sentence; for example, **Eating is something we all have to do to stay alive, <u>but</u> it is also high on most people's list of favourite things to do.**
- words or ideas in sentences; for example, **saliva <u>and</u> bacteria**.

Let's find them!

Tip!

Here is a list of **conjunctions**: after, although, and, as, because, before, but, either, if, neither, nor, once, or, so, unless, until, when, whenever, whereas, whether, while and yet.

Use the list to find seven **conjunctions** in the text. You may use the ones in bold.

Be careful! Sometimes conjunctions are placed at the beginning of a sentence!

 _____

Unit 8: Chew on this!   43

2. _____ 5. _____
3. _____ 6. _____
4. _____ 7. _____

Let's go to the next step!

Complete each sentence with a **conjunction** from the box. Use each word once.

| until | but | if | after | once | because | so |

1. I always brush my teeth _____ I eat lollies.
2. _____ an adult loses a tooth, it won't grow back again.
3. I look after my teeth _____ I don't want them to decay.
4. He has a sore tooth, _____ he won't go to the dentist.
5. The dentist found a cavity in one of my teeth, _____ he filled it.
6. I kept on brushing my teeth _____ I was satisfied that they were clean.
7. He said he would go to the dentist _____ his tooth continued to ache.

Let's aim high now!

Cross out the **conjunction** in brackets that does not complete the sentence correctly. For example: I'll go to the dentist (when/yet/if) I have the time.

1. I didn't know (if/until/whether) he would take me to the dentist.
2. The dentist (and/nor/or) her nurse will be waiting for me at the clinic.
3. I sit very still (once/while/yet) the dentist is working on my teeth.
4. I get frightened (when/whereas/whenever) I have to go to the dentist.
5. My mother spoke to the dentist (although/before/after) my appointment.
6. She doesn't like going to the dentist, (if/yet/but) she visits him every six months.
7. I made an appointment to see the dentist (unless/because/as) I was having trouble with my teeth.

No more drilling!

Most of us are terrified **of** dentists—that is, when they have a drill in their hands! But going to the dentist may soon be a much less frightening experience. Imagine being able to grow a new tooth when the old one wears out. Or never getting tooth decay in the first place!

Scientists are experimenting on animals to develop special substances that do just that, and they are hoping that their experiments on humans will be as successful. They are also predicting that one day they will be able to heal a damaged tooth simply by spraying a special substance on it.

For most of us, that day can't come too soon. In the meantime, the best way to keep tooth decay at bay is to keep using that toothbrush!

*This is another **information leaflet**. The author uses **prepositions** to show the relationship between nouns or pronouns and other words while informing us about dental care in the future.*

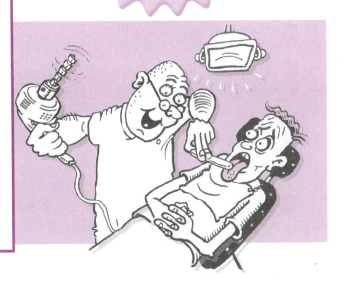

Prepositions are words that show relationships between nouns or pronouns and other words; for example, **of** shows the relationship between the adjective *terrified* and the noun *dentists*.

 ## Let's find them!

Use the list to help you find seven different **prepositions** in the text and then write them in the spaces. You may also use the words in bold.

1. _____
2. _____
3. _____
4. _____
5. _____
6. _____
7. _____

Tip!

Here is a list of **prepositions**: about, above, across, against, along, among, around, at, before, behind, below, beneath, beside, beyond, by, down, during, except, for, from, in, inside, into, near, of, off, on, over, past, since, to, towards, through, under, up, with, within and **without**.

Unit 8: Chew on this!

Let's go to the next step!

Complete each sentence with a **preposition** from the box. Use each word once.

| through | under | of | in | past | for | near | to | on | during | from | against | since |

1. The dentist tied a bib _____ my chin.

2. The dentist's clinic is _____ our house.

3. My tooth started to ache _____ the night.

4. I could see the dentist _____ the gap _____ the wall.

5. I leaned _____ the wall while I waited _____ the dentist.

6. I walk _____ the dentist's clinic _____ my way home _____ school.

7. I haven't been _____ the dentist _____ the beginning _____ last year.

Let's aim high now!

Cross out the **preposition** in brackets that does not complete the sentence correctly.
For example: The little girl put her tooth (in/of/on) her bag.

1. The dentist walked (towards/down/around) his chair.

2. We found the little boy's tooth (behind/beneath/to) the bed.

3. The dentist (since/from/at) the clinic says I have strong teeth.

4. I walked (without/along/across) the street to the dentists' rooms.

5. I've heard (of/off/about) the man who can lift a bicycle with his teeth.

6. He told her that the tooth fairy lives (except/beyond/above) the clouds.

7. Carla put her tooth (in/through/inside) her slipper for the tooth fairy to find.

Let's put it together now!

This student isn't sure where to write these **conjunctions** and **prepositions** in this section of his article. Help him fill them in.

| and | for | from | on | but | between | or |

Most people can lift very light objects with their teeth, _____ some people have incredibly strong teeth and can lift much heavier loads. A man _____ India, known as the Tooth Warrior _____ The Man with the Diamond Teeth, can lift a bicycle with his teeth! Another man recently broke the world record _____ carrying the heaviest load the longest distance using only his teeth! He clenched a table weighing 12 kg _____ his jaws _____ carried it for almost 12 m. To add to the table's weight, a girl weighing 50 kg sat _____ it!

Let's have fun!

Adult humans have thirty-two teeth—sixteen in the upper jaw and sixteen in the lower jaw. Cap this person's teeth with the **conjunctions** and **prepositions** floating about in her mouth. Write each conjunction on a tooth in the upper jaw, and each preposition on a tooth in the lower jaw. When you have finished, every tooth should have a conjunction or a preposition. Use the lists of conjunctions and prepositions in this unit to help you.

by	either	to	because	but	near	or	over
on	for	until	after	from	without	while	up
yet	nor	unless	and	if	so	during	although
when	at	about	with	once	in	along	into

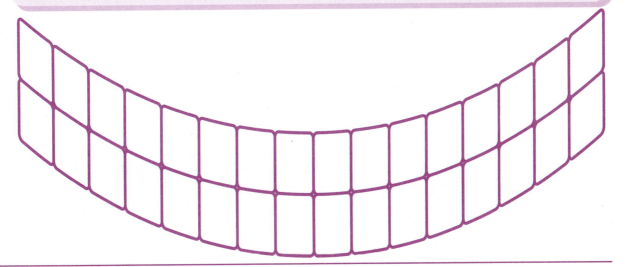

Unit 8: Chew on this!

Let's have a test!

In questions 1–8, which word completes each sentence correctly?

1 A shark gets new teeth _____ it loses its old ones.
- but
- when
- either
- or

2 Both giraffes _____ humans have thirty-two teeth.
- yet
- nor
- and
- if

3 I brush my teeth regularly _____ I want them to be healthy.
- because
- until
- unless
- while

4 I told him to brush his teeth, _____ he ignored me.
- once
- whenever
- after
- but

5 I bought a toothbrush _____ soft bristles.
- with
- for
- since
- from

6 The boy has braces _____ his teeth.
- in
- on
- by
- of

7 I brush my teeth _____ two minutes.
- from
- at
- to
- for

8 When playing sport, protect your teeth _____ injury.
- for
- to
- from
- during

Let's write now!

Look in books or on the Internet for information on teeth and gums, and then write an **information leaflet** giving information about the different types of teeth and/or advice on oral hygiene. Use **conjunctions** and **prepositions** in your information leaflet.

Unit 9 — Striking it rich!

Focus
Adjectival and adverbial phrases; noun phrases; commas

Digging for gold

Gold is a beautiful precious metal **with a shiny, yellow appearance**. Although it is very heavy, it is soft enough to be hammered **into thin shapes**. A single gram of gold can be beaten into a sheet one square metre in size. For this reason, it has been used for thousands of years to make jewellery and ornaments. It is also associated with wealth and plays an important role in our monetary system.

Gold is found in rock beneath the ground. Sometimes it is washed to the surface and ends up in streams and dry riverbeds. To get to the gold under the ground, big mining companies dig into the earth and bring the gold-bearing rock to the surface, where it is crushed and the metal is extracted. The gold is then melted and formed into bars.

by Jesse

This is an **explanation**. An explanation tells why something happens or how it works. Jesse uses **adjectival phrases** to give more information about nouns and **adverbial phrases** to give more information about verbs in his explanation of how gold is mined.

Phrases are groups of words in a sentence. They do not usually contain a verb.
- **Adjectival phrases** do the work of adjectives—they give us more information about nouns; for example, **with a shiny, yellow appearance** tells us more about the noun *gold*.
- **Adverbial phrases** do the work of **adverbs**—they give us more information about verbs; for example, **into thin shapes** tells us more about how gold is *hammered*.

Let's find them!

Tip!
Adjectival and adverbial phrases usually start with a preposition.

Find these **phrases** in the text and state whether they are doing the work of an adjective or an adverb.

1. of gold _____
2. into a sheet _____
3. in size _____
4. for thousands of years _____

Unit 9: Striking it rich!   49

5. in our monetary system _____
6. to the surface _____
7. under the ground _____

Let's go to the next step!

Underline the **adjectival** and **adverbial phrases** in these sentences. In each case, state which type of phrase it is. For example: The gold bangles <u>on her arm</u> jingle when she moves. _____*adjectival*_____

> **Tip!** Find the preposition in each sentence—that will help you find the **phrase**.

1. Australia exports gold around the world. _____
2. The gold bars were delivered to the bank. _____
3. The opals in the box were blue and green. _____
4. The diamond necklace cost a lot of money. _____
5. The gold nugget was lying beside the stream. _____
6. My mother bought an opal ring from that shop. _____
7. The treasures beneath the earth are often hard to find. _____

Let's aim high now!

Complete each sentence with a **phrase** from the box. State whether it is an **adjectival** or an **adverbial** phrase. For example, People <u>with lots of money</u> often buy expensive jewellery. _____*adjectival*_____

> **Tip!** Reading through the sentences before you start will help you work out which phrases go where.

from the mine	for many days	without a price tag
in her ring	from falling rocks	for a mining company
	inside a safe	

1. The stone _____ is an emerald. _____
2. My father works _____. _____
3. The miner panned _____ before he found gold. _____
4. A man _____ showed us how to pan for gold. _____
5. The ring _____ is probably very expensive. _____
6. The jeweller keeps his most precious items _____. _____
7. The miner wore a hard hat to protect his head _____. _____

Life on the goldfields

In 1851, Edward Hargraves discovered gold at Ophir in New South Wales. Shortly afterwards, gold was discovered in Victoria. **Thousands of people from Australia and overseas** flocked to the goldfields. All hoped to make their fortunes; very few did.

Life on the goldfields was extremely difficult. At first there were no **roads, shops or houses**. People had to bring their own picks, shovels and any other equipment they needed with them, and the only way they could get there was on horseback, by cart or on foot. Living on the goldfields was like living on a huge campsite. There were tents dotted all around the diggings. Eventually, more permanent dwellings of wood, bark and canvas replaced the tents, and stores, hotels and theatres popped up. Today, many of those early gold-mining settlements are thriving towns and cities.

by Kate

> This is a **factual recount**. Remember: a recount tells about things that have already happened. In her recount about life on the goldfields, Kate uses **noun phrases** to tell who or what is involved in the sentence and **commas** to separate items in a list.

Noun phrases are groups of words that are built around a noun. They tell us who or what is involved in the sentence; for example: **Thousands of people from Australia and overseas** is a group of words that is built around the noun **people**.

This phrase also tells us who flocked to the goldfields.

Rule! **Commas** are used to separate items in a list; for example, **roads, shops or houses**.

Let's find them!

Tip! The last two words in a list are usually separated by the conjunctions **or** or **and**, not by a **comma**.

Find the **noun phrase** in the text that tells us

1. what was extremely difficult. _____
2. what was like being on a huge campsite. _____
3. what eventually replaced the tents. _____
4. what many of those early gold-mining settlements are today. _____

Unit 9: **Striking it rich!**

Find three lists in the text and write them in the spaces. Don't use the list in bold, and don't forget the **commas**!

5 _____

6 _____

7 _____

Let's go to the next step!

Fill in the missing **commas** in these sentences.

1 Gold silver and platinum are precious metals.

2 In winter it was cold wet and windy on the goldfields.

3 The miners bought meat milk eggs and vegetables from a local farmer.

4 A lady wearing a diamond necklace bracelet and earrings came to see us.

4 People from Europe Asia Africa and America came to the Australian goldfields.

5 While digging for opals, the miner found some old coins bones and bits of metal.

7 The jeweller showed me a ring set with diamonds rubies emeralds and sapphires.

Let's aim high now!

These sentences have been divided into three parts. Put them back together by shading the parts that go together the same colour. The first one has been done for you.

Tip!
Do the obvious ones first!

Noun phrase	Verb	Noun phrase
1 The miner	destroyed	a beautiful gold necklace.
2 The boat from Europe	designed	the gold to melt.
3 Some lucky fortune hunters	provides	supplies for the gold mines.
4 The raging bushfire	enjoyed	work for many people.
5 The famous jeweller	carried	panning for gold.
6 The new gold mine	caused	large amounts of gold.
7 The heat from the furnace	found	the miners' huts.

Let's put it together now!

This student has used **adjectival**, **adverbial** and **noun phrases** in his recount, but he has left out some important words. He has also left out a **comma**. Fill in the missing words and punctuation for him.

| to | in | gold | mines | from | of |

Early _____ miners used a pan to extract gold _____ streams and dry riverbeds. They would scoop up some gravel add a bit of water and then move the pan about gently. The gold would sink _____ the bottom. Some old gold _____ have become tourist attractions where people can experience what life was like for those early diggers. Visitors are shown how to pan for gold. They are even allowed to keep any flakes _____ gold that they might find. I have a bottle with two little flakes of gold _____ it!

Let's have fun!

Match the lists below with the pictures. Notice that the clue that accompanies each picture is a phrase!

| diamonds, rubies and sapphires | dollars, cents and pounds |
| necklaces, rings and earrings | coal, oil and gas |

a box of jewels

energy from fossil fuels

savings in the bank

a bracelet with gemstones

Unit 9: Striking it rich!

Let's have a test!

In questions 1–3, which phrase completes the sentence correctly?

1 The box _____ is in the safe.
- ○ of gold coins
- ○ for gold coins
- ○ from gold coins
- ○ near gold coins

2 The precious stones _____ are worth a lot of money.
- ○ of her collection
- ○ in her collection
- ○ on her collection
- ○ into her collection

3 The miner sold the gold nugget _____.
- ○ to a jeweller
- ○ in a jeweller
- ○ from a jeweller
- ○ at a jeweller

4 Which phrase does **not** complete this sentence correctly?

They built the houses _____.
- ○ near the mine
- ○ beside the mine
- ○ behind the mine
- ○ between the mine

In questions 5–6, where should the commas go in each sentence?

5 We get energy from coal oil and gas.

6 Crystals precious stones precious metals and fossil fuels come from the earth.

7 In which sentence has the noun phrase been written correctly?
- ○ He bought a large, round barrel of oil.
- ○ He bought many large, round barrel of oil.
- ○ He bought those large, round barrel of oil.
- ○ He bought an large, round barrel of oil.

8 Which sequence of words completes this sentence correctly?

_____ large truck _____ steel doors transported the gold.
- ○ A, of
- ○ An, with
- ○ A, with
- ○ An, of

Let's write now!

Look in books or on the Internet for information on the discovery of opals in Australia, or find out more about life on the goldfields in the 1850s. Write a **recount** about the topic you have chosen. Use **adjectival**, **adverbial** and **noun phrases** in your recount, as well as **commas** to separate items in lists.

54   Year 6 Grammar and Punctuation Workbook

Unit 10 Natural disasters

> ★ **Focus**
> Sentences: subjects, verbs and objects; active and passive voice

Natural disasters in Australia

In her poem *My Country*, Dorothea McKellar describes Australia as a land of 'droughts and flooding rains'. The extreme weather conditions that are responsible for these disasters cause immense damage to life and property. Tropical cyclones in the north flatten coastal towns and crops in minutes. Heavy rainfall turns creeks into raging torrents that sweep away everything in their path. Bushfires destroy forests and human settlements. **Droughts kill sheep, cattle and other livestock.**

We can't change the weather patterns that cause these natural disasters. However, we can make sure that we don't become the victims of these events. We shouldn't build houses too close to river banks, and we should plan carefully when building in forested areas. Most importantly, we should always obey instructions to evacuate our homes before cyclones, floods or bushfires reach us.

by Lindsay

> This is a **description**. A description creates a mind picture of a person, place, object or event. Lindsay uses **sentences** containing **subjects**, **verbs** and **objects** to describe the natural disasters that occur in Australia.

In Unit 5 you learnt that a sentence consists of two parts: a **subject** and a **predicate**, which contains the **verb**; for example, **Droughts** (subject) **kill livestock** (predicate).

This sentence can also be divided into a **subject**, **verb** and **object**; for example, *Droughts* (subject) *kill* (verb) *livestock* (object).

The subject in a sentence
- is the person, animal or thing that does the action.
- comes before the verb; for example, <u>Droughts</u> kill livestock.

The object in a sentence
- is the person, animal or thing that has the action done to them.
- comes after the verb; for example, Droughts kill <u>livestock</u>.

Let's find them!

Find the **subjects** that perform these actions in the text.

① the person who <u>describes</u> Australia in a poem _____

Unit 10: **Natural disasters** 55

② the events that <u>flatten</u> coastal towns and crops _____

③ the event that <u>turns</u> creeks into raging torrents _____

Now find the **objects** that have these actions done to them.

④ the things that bushfires <u>destroy</u> _____

⑤ the things we <u>can't change</u> _____

⑥ the things we <u>shouldn't build</u> close to river banks _____

⑦ the things we <u>should obey</u> _____

Let's go to the next step!

State whether the underlined words are the **subject**, **verb** or **object** in the sentence.
For example: The heavy rain stripped <u>the leaves</u> off the trees. _____*object*_____

① The tsunami <u>changed</u> the shape of the shoreline. _____

② <u>Tremors</u> shook the earth for days after the earthquake. _____

③ Droughts cause <u>great suffering</u> to the people on the land. _____

④ The tsunami destroyed <u>the island</u> and caused many deaths. _____

⑤ The cyclone smashed <u>the little boats in the harbour</u>. _____

⑥ People in town <u>gave</u> the flood victims shelter for the night. _____

⑦ <u>The large tree behind our house</u> fell during the storm. _____

Let's aim high now!

Underline the **subjects** and circle the **objects** in these sentences.
For example: <u>The smoke from the bushfire</u> damaged (his lungs)

① The rising waters covered our garden.

② The wild winds blew down power lines.

③ The bushfire scorched our neighbour's fence.

④ The large wave carried away cars and houses.

⑤ The rumbling volcano frightened the townspeople.

⑥ The fire destroyed the habitats of birds and other wildlife.

⑦ A hailstone the size of a tennis ball broke one of our windows.

56   Year 6 Grammar and Punctuation Workbook

The Boxing Day tsunami

On December 26th 2004, an earthquake erupted off the coast of Sumatra. It caused powerful waves across the Indian Ocean.

Parts of Indonesia were devastated by the huge waves an hour after the eruption. A short while later, beaches in southern Thailand were hit. **The tsunami then washed over the coasts of India and Sri Lanka. A passenger train in Sri Lanka was lifted into the air.** Most of the 1500 people on board were killed.

The waves continued eastwards to the coast of Africa. Along the way, they destroyed coastal areas in the Maldives. Finally, six hours after the eruption, the tsunami ended its journey in East Africa.

The Boxing Day tsunami caused great suffering. Homes and buildings were destroyed. Water supplies and other services were disrupted. But worst of all, more than 200 000 people lost their lives.

by Sheraan

This is a **factual recount**. Remember: a recount retells events that have already happened. In his recount, Sheraan uses the **active** and **passive voice** to tell about the devastation caused by the Boxing Day tsunami.

Voice is used in connection with verbs.
- The **active voice** is when the person or thing doing the action is the **subject** of the sentence; for example, **The tsunami** then washed over the coasts of India and Sri Lanka.
- The **passive voice** is when the person or thing having the action done to them is the **subject** of the sentence; for example, **A passenger train in Sri Lanka** was lifted into the air.

Rule!

Notice how the **subjects** and **objects** change places in these sentences:
- *The tsunami* **(subject)** *destroyed* **(verb)** *the island* **(object)**. (active voice)
- *The island* **(subject)** *was destroyed by the tsunami*. (passive voice)

Let's find them!

State whether these sentences have been written in the **active** or **passive voice**.

1. Parts of Indonesia were devastated by the huge waves. _____

2. Beaches in southern Thailand were hit a short while later. _____

3. Most of the 1500 people on board were killed. _____

Tip!

Sometimes when we know who or what is causing the action, we don't have to include that information; for example, **The island was destroyed.**

Unit 10: **Natural disasters**

4. The waves destroyed coastal areas in the Maldives. _____

5. The Boxing Day tsunami caused great suffering. _____

6. Homes and buildings were destroyed. _____

7. Water supplies and other services were disrupted. _____

Let's go to the next step!

Complete these sentences by filling in the **verb** or **verb group** from the box.

| are being | been | to be | is being | were | had been | will be | was |

1. Right now, people _____ airlifted to safety.
2. In future, houses _____ built from stronger materials.
3. Many roofs _____ blown off when the wind picked up.
4. The electricity supply to the town has already _____ cut off.
5. The town that _____ devastated by the floods _____ rebuilt as we speak.
6. People's lives continue _____ disrupted by natural disasters such as floods and droughts.
7. The last time I was in the town, I noticed that houses _____ built right next to the river.

Let's aim high now!

Rewrite these sentences in the **passive voice** by starting them with the underlined words.

For example: The waves washed away the beach. *The beach was washed away by the waves.*

1. The tornado lifted cars into the air. _____

2. A lightning strike caused the bushfire. _____

3. The heavy rains cut short our holiday. _____

4. Cyclones destroyed the farmers' crops. _____

5. Large hailstones caused the dents in our car. _____

Let's put it together now!

This student has used both the **active** and **passive voice** while telling about an earthquake. He has written seven **verbs** incorrectly. Use a red pen to make the corrections for him.

On 22nd February 2011, the city of Christchurch were hit by a 6.3 magnitude earthquake. It causes widespread damage because it occurred so close to the city. Altogether, 185 people killed, making it the second worst natural disaster in New Zealand's history. It has also being very expensive to repair the damage caused by the earthquake. When the earthquake striked, many people come to the aid of those who was trapped, including ordinary citizens.

Let's have fun!

The **sentences** contain clues in brackets to help you fill in the missing letters in this puzzle.

1. The town was completely (another word for ruined) by the tornado.
   d ◯ s ◯ r ◯◯◯◯

2. Lots of (small areas of land surrounded by water) were in the path of the cyclone.
   i ◯ l ◯◯ d ◯

3. When the large wave appeared, the air was filled with the (high pitched sounds) of hundreds of people.
   s ◯◯ e ◯ m ◯

4. Humans as well as (other living creatures) lost their homes during the cyclone.
   a ◯ i ◯ a ◯◯

5. The earthquake opened up large cracks in the (places we drive on).
   s ◯ r ◯ e ◯◯

6. The (very large wave) swept over the village.
   t ◯◯◯ a ◯ i

7. The (violent shaking of the ground) caused lots of damage.
   e ◯◯◯ h ◯◯ a ◯◯

8. The cyclone caused strong winds that (another word for tore) through the town.
   r ◯◯ p ◯ d

Unit 10: **Natural disasters**

Let's have a test!

1 Which sentence is **incorrect**?
- ○ There is a drought in the country.
- ○ It get worse every month.
- ○ The sheep and cattle are dying.
- ○ I hope it ends soon.

2 Which word completes this sentence correctly?

The wind has _____ down the tree.
- ○ blow
- ○ blows
- ○ blown
- ○ blew

3 Which is the subject in this sentence?

The houses near the river got flooded.
- ○ houses
- ○ The houses
- ○ the river
- ○ The houses near the river

4 Which is the object in this sentence?

An earthquake struck the small island.
- ○ An earthquake
- ○ earthquake
- ○ the small island
- ○ island

5 Which sentence is in the passive voice?
- ○ The storm damaged the power lines.
- ○ The wind blew down the flagpole.
- ○ The lightning struck the building.
- ○ The flagpole was blown down by the wind.

6 Which word or words can be left out of this sentence?

The old church was destroyed by the earthquake.
- ○ by the earthquake
- ○ the earthquake
- ○ by
- ○ destroyed

In questions 7–8, which words complete the sentence correctly?

7 Many islanders _____ by falling bricks.
- ○ have been
- ○ been hurt
- ○ have being hurt
- ○ have been hurt

8 Many buildings _____ the earthquake.
- ○ were destroyed
- ○ were destroyed by
- ○ was destroyed
- ○ was destroyed by

Let's write now!

Look in books or on the Internet for information about a natural disaster that has caused a lot of damage, and then write a **factual recount** about it. Use the **active** and **passive voice** in your recount.

Unit 11 Robots

★ **Focus**
Direct speech; speech marks; indirect speech

Do robots help people?

"Dad, do you think it's a good idea that robots are doing work that people used to do?" asked Jacqui.

Dad scratched his chin and said, "That depends."

"What do you mean?" asked Jacqui.

"It's good that robots are able to do boring or dangerous jobs," said Dad.

"You mean like the robot they've sent to Mars," interrupted Jacqui.

"Exactly!" exclaimed Dad. "But on the other hand, robots are putting people out of work."

"So," mused Jacqui, "robots are like … what's that saying again?"

"Like a double-edged sword," said Dad. "They have their good points and their bad points."

This is a **discussion**. A discussion looks at both sides of an argument. The author uses **direct speech** with **speech marks** to show the exact words that Jacqui and her dad use while discussing the advantages and disadvantages of robots.

Direct speech
- quotes the exact words that someone says in a text; for example, **"Dad, do you think it's a good idea that robots are doing work that people used to do?"** are Jacqui's exact words.
- always has **speech** or **quotation marks** around the spoken words; for example, "Dad, do you think it's a good idea that robots are doing work that people used to do?"

When someone starts speaking for the first time, the first word they say always starts with a capital letter, even if it comes after a comma; for example, **Dad scratched his chin and said, "That depends."**

Let's find them!

Find these sentences in the text and fill in the missing **punctuation marks**.

① What do you mean asked Jacqui.

Tip!
The punctuation that comes at the end of what someone says goes inside the speech mark; for example,

Unit 11: **Robots**

2. It's good that robots are able to do boring or dangerous jobs said Dad.

3. You mean like the robot they've sent to Mars interrupted Jacqui.

4. Exactly exclaimed Dad.

5. But on the other hand, robots are putting people out of work

6. So mused Jacqui robots are like … what's that saying again

7. Like a double-edged sword said Dad They have their good points and their bad points

Let's go to the next step!

Underline the **actual words** that the people say in these sentences.
For example: "<u>I wish I had my own robot</u>," said Jordan.

1. "Is this robot powered by batteries?" asked Paul.

2. "If only I had a robot to carry out the garbage," whined Rory.

3. "One good thing about robots," said Joe, "is that they never get sick!"

4. "This robot is made from metal and plastic," said the science teacher.

5. "If you want to know how to build a robot," said Neil, "watch this video."

6. "I think that people who can build robots are very clever," commented Aunt Maud.

7. "One problem with robots is that they are unable to think for themselves," said Will, "but maybe that's a good thing."

Let's aim high now!

Use a red pen to fill in the missing **speech marks** in these sentences.

1. Many science fiction books are about robots, said Mr Marks.

2. Have you ever built a robot? asked Jules, because I haven't.

3. Look what I made in robotics! exclaimed Olivia, holding up a small robot.

4. I went to see the movie about robots, announced Hilda, and it was scary.

5. The teacher said, Many robots are used in factories to build things like cars.

6. The boss exclaimed, The best thing about robots is that they never complain!

7. I think robots can really help humans, said Ms Scott, as long as we use them properly.

Dave's speech

Dave told the class that it was really easy to build a robot. He said that he built his first robot using a kit he bought in a hobby shop. He said the instructions were very easy to follow. He explained to us how he put the parts together and programmed the robot. He then showed us how he could make the robot move forwards, backwards and turn corners. I asked him how long it took him to build the robot. Dave replied that the first one took him a few days to put together. He added that he'd built two more robots since then. These, he said, had taken him much less time to make.

by Marcus

This is a **recount**. Remember: a recount tells about things that have already happened. Marcus uses **indirect speech** to tell what his classmate, Dave, said about building a robot without using his exact words.

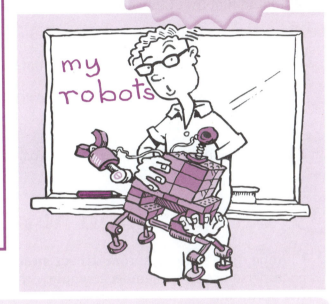

Indirect or **reported speech**
- tells what someone said without using their exact words; for example, **Dave told the class that it was really easy to build a robot.** These are not Dave's exact words. His exact words would have been: "It is really easy to build a robot."
- does not have **speech marks**.

Let's find them!

Underline the sentence in the text that is similar in meaning to each of these sentences. Use a different colour for each sentence and match the colours to the sentences below; for example, place a blue tick next to the first sentence and underline its matching sentence in blue.

1. "I built my first robot using a kit I bought in a hobby shop," said Dave.
2. Dave said, "The instructions are very easy to follow."
3. "This is how I put the parts together and programmed the robot," explained Dave.
4. "How long did it take you to build the robot?" asked Marcus.
5. "The first one took me a few days to put together," replied Dave.
6. "I've built two more robots since then," Dave added.
7. "These have taken me much less time to make," said Dave.

Unit 11: **Robots**

Let's go to the next step!

Complete these sentences by choosing the past tense **verb** in brackets. Cross out the one that is wrong.

For example: Paula said that she (~~will~~/would) show me how to build a robot.

1. They said that we (could/can) try out the new robot.
2. I told him that I (have/had) already worked out how to build the robot.
3. I said I (would/will) help him build the robot if he (wants/wanted) me to.
4. Lee announced proudly that her robot (has/had) taken its first few steps!
5. My friend said that he (sees/saw) a very advanced robot at a science fair.
6. Flynn said that I (should/shall) read the instructions before building the robot.
7. She said that the robot ASIMO (is/was) the most advanced robot in the world.

Let's aim high now!

Change these sentences from **direct speech** to **indirect speech** by filling in what each person said. Remember to change the tense of the verb and, where necessary, the pronoun.

For example: "What can your robot do?" asked Margie.
   Margie asked _____what my robot could do_____.

1. "I love playing with my robot," said Anna.

   Anna said that _____.

2. "It is my brother's robot," said Samantha.

   Samantha said that _____.

3. "I want a robot for my birthday," said Barry.

   Barry said that _____.

4. "I don't know how to build a robot," said Max.

   Max said that _____.

5. "We won't finish the robot today," said the boys.

   The boys said that _____.

6. "I have learnt how to program a robot," said Richard.

   Richard said that _____.

7. "Which robot are you going to buy?" James asked John.

   James asked John _____.

Let's put it together now!

This student has made the following mistakes in these sentences: he has written the underlined words in the wrong **tense** and he has made five **punctuation** errors. Use a red pen to make the corrections for him.

Mum, if you could buy a robot to help you around the house, would you get one"? asked Kevin.

Mum replied that she had never really thought about it, but probably <u>will</u>, if it wasn't too expensive.

"Which jobs would you get the robot to do?" asked Kevin.

"Well", replied Mum, the first thing I'd program it to do would be to clean your room"!

Kevin said that <u>is</u> fine with him.

Let's have fun!

The computer inside this robot has short-circuited and the **punctuation** in the sentences coming up on the robot's screen has jumped about. Write the sentences correctly on the lines below. Make sure you use all the punctuation marks.

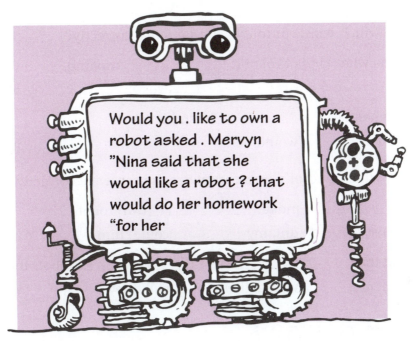

Unit 11: **Robots**

Let's have a test!

In questions 1–3, which sentence has been punctuated correctly?

1
- ○ "Are robots fun to play with?" asked Stuart.
- ○ "Are robots fun to play with? asked Stuart."
- ○ "Are robots fun to play with," asked Stuart.
- ○ "Are robots fun to play with!" asked Stuart.

2
- ○ "This is my new robot," said Jake, "and that's my old one".
- ○ "This is my new robot", said Jake, "and that's my old one."
- ○ "This is my new robot," said Jake, "and that's my old one."
- ○ "This is my new robot," said Jake, "And that's my old one."

3
- ○ Dad exclaimed, "What a magnificent robot"!
- ○ Dad exclaimed "What a magnificent robot!"
- ○ Dad exclaimed. "What a magnificent robot!"
- ○ Dad exclaimed, "What a magnificent robot!"

4 Where do the speech marks go in this sentence?

That robot scares me ,   said Jill .
  ↑   ↑   ↑↑   ↑
  ○   ○   ○○   ○

In questions 5–6, which word completes the sentence correctly?

5 Jodie asked me what kind of robot I _____ making.
- ○ am   ○ are   ○ was   ○ were

6 I asked him when he _____ finish his robot.
- ○ will   ○ would   ○ was   ○ is

In questions 7–8, which pair of words completes the sentence correctly?

7 He said I _____ make _____ own robot.
- ○ should, her   ○ am, my   ○ could, him   ○ should, my

8 The boys said they _____ try out _____ robots that afternoon.
- ○ would, them   ○ would, their   ○ will, they   ○ will, us

Let's write now!

Look in books or on the Internet for information on robots and choose one of the following.

1. Write a **discussion** in which two people discuss the advantages and disadvantages of robots. Use **direct speech** with **speech marks** in your discussion.

2. Write a **recount** in which you tell about a time you saw, built or played with a robot. Use **reported speech** in your recount.

Unit 12 Animals with armour

★ Focus
Clauses: simple, compound and complex sentences

Echidnas

The echidna is native to Australia. It is a small animal, but it is covered with spines. These help to protect it from predators.

The echidna has some unusual characteristics. It is a mammal, yet it lays eggs! Its mouth is very small and it has no teeth. Instead, it has a long, sticky tongue that it uses to catch ants and termites.

The female echidna lays a single egg and keeps it safe in her pouch. The young echidna, called a puggle, hatches ten days later. It remains in the pouch for about seven weeks while it develops spines. The mother then moves it to a burrow. She continues to suckle it for seven months.

Unbelievably, these small animals can survive for up to fifty years!

by Lien

This is an **information report**. An information report provides information and facts. Lien uses mainly **simple** and **compound sentences** to provide information and facts about the echidna.

Sentences can be divided into clauses.

Clauses are groups of words that contain
- a complete idea or message.
- a verb or verb group.

Main clauses contain the main idea or message.

Simple sentences contain one complete idea and one verb or verb group. They contain one main clause; for example, **The echidna <u>is</u> native to Australia.**

Compound sentences have two or more main clauses joined by a conjunction; for example, **It is a small animal, <u>but</u> it is covered with spines**.

Let's find them!

Find these sentences in the text and state whether they are **simple** or **compound sentences**.

① The echidna has some unusual characteristics.

Tip!
The conjunctions that join **simple sentences** to make **compound sentences** are **and, but, yet, so, or** and **nor**.

Unit 12: **Animals with armour**

2. It is a mammal, yet it lays eggs! _____

3. Its mouth is very small and it has no teeth. _____

4. The female echidna lays a single egg and keeps it safe in her pouch. _____

5. The mother then moves it to a burrow. _____

6. She continues to suckle it for seven months. _____

Let's go to the next step!

> **Tip!**
> A comma usually separates clauses that are joined by **yet**, **but**, **nor**, **or** and **so**.

Complete each sentence with a **conjunction** from the tip box on page 67. Use each word at least once.

1. The tortoise was badly injured, _____ it survived.

2. I don't want a pet crab, _____ do I want a pet turtle.

3. I would pat an echidna, _____ I wouldn't touch a porcupine!

4. Would you like a pet crab, _____ would you prefer a pet turtle?

5. Tortoises have hard, thick shells, _____ they are well protected.

6. I have seen echidnas in the zoo _____ I've seen them in the wild.

7. We wanted to hold the puggles, _____ the zookeeper wouldn't let us.

Let's aim high now!

> **Tip!**
> Don't repeat nouns when you can replace them with pronouns, and don't repeat words unnecessarily; for example, Snails live on land. Snails live in the sea./Snails live on land <u>and</u> in the sea.

Use conjunctions to join these **simple sentences** to make **compound sentences**.

1. Birds have scales on their legs. Birds have scales on their heads.
_____

2. Most fish have scales for protection. Early fish had hard, bony plates.
_____

3. Hedgehogs sleep under bushes. Hedgehogs sleep in holes in the ground.
_____

4. The tortoise felt threatened by the dog. The tortoise retreated into its shell.
_____

5. Hedgehogs are mainly nocturnal. Hedgehogs can be active during the day.
_____

6. Some dinosaurs had spikes on their bodies. Others were covered in plates.
_____

7. The echidna came out of the burrow. The echidna started walking towards us.
_____

The saltwater crocodile

The saltwater crocodile is an excellent example of an animal with armour! This large reptile, which is found in northern Australia and Asia, is covered in tough, bony scales.

Although saltwater crocodiles spend most of their time in swamps and estuaries, they sometimes travel far out to sea. **When they are hungry, they will eat whatever is on offer.** They've even been known to eat sharks!

The female saltwater crocodile, who is a fiercely protective mother, lays her eggs in the wet season. She guards them until they hatch. Even after they have hatched, she continues to keep a watchful eye on the baby crocodiles for the first few weeks of their life.

Although other carnivores often eat baby saltwater crocodiles, the adults have no natural predators. The greatest threat to their survival as a species is human activity.

by Bruno

This is another **information report**. Bruno uses mainly **complex sentences** to provide information about the saltwater crocodile.

So far you have learnt that a simple sentence has one main clause and a compound sentence has two or more main clauses.

Complex sentences have
- one main clause that contains the main idea or message of the sentence.
- at least one other clause that contains a verb but which cannot stand on its own. This is called a **dependent clause**; for example, **When they are hungry, they will eat whatever is on offer.** In this sentence, the main clause is *they will eat whatever is on offer* and the dependent clause is *When they are hungry*.

Dependent clauses can be introduced by a conjunction or a pronoun.

Rule! These are some of the conjunctions that introduce dependent clauses: **after**, **although**, **as**, **because**, **before**, **if**, **once**, **since**, **though**, **unless**, **until**, **when**, **whenever** and **while**.

Pronouns that introduce dependent clauses are **that**, **which**, **who**, **whom** and **whose**.

Let's find them!

Tip! These pronouns are called **relative pronouns**.

Find these clauses in the text and state whether they are **main** or **dependent clauses**.

1. which is found in northern Australia and Asia _____
2. they sometimes travel far out to sea _____

Unit 12: **Animals with armour**

3 who is a fiercely protective mother _____

4 until they hatch _____

5 she continues to keep a watchful eye on the baby crocodiles for the first few weeks of their life _____

6 Although other carnivores often eat baby saltwater crocodiles _____

Let's go to the next step!

Complete each of these sentences with a **dependent clause** from the box.

> because it was too small
> Although the snake is harmless
> which is very small
> When I approached it
> with whom I watched the documentary
> once I've fed my pet turtle
> If you see a saltwater crocodile on the river bank

1 _____, the crab quickly scuttled away.

2 I will make myself a sandwich _____.

3 _____, I won't touch it.

4 The shell, _____, must have belonged to a sea snail.

5 _____, don't try to pat it!

6 The fisherman threw the lobster back _____.

7 The boy _____ knows a lot about animals with armour.

Let's aim high now!

> **Tip!**
> The **dependent clauses** may appear at the beginning, in the middle or at the end of the sentence.

Underline the **main clauses** and put a box around the **dependent clauses** in these sentences.

1 If a lobster loses a claw or leg, it will grow a new one.

2 The porcupine, whose body is covered in spines, is a rodent.

3 The tortoise won't emerge from its shell while it feels threatened.

4 I saw a large saltwater crocodile when I went to the Northern Territory.

5 The crocodile, which was enormous, suddenly jumped out of the water.

6 Yesterday I met a man who had been attacked by a saltwater crocodile.

7 Before we visited the reptile park, I watched a documentary about crocodiles.

Let's put it together now!

This student has left out the following **conjunctions** and **relative pronouns** in her information report about the hermit crab. Help her to fill them in correctly.

| if | which | but | because | when | or | and |

Hermit crabs, _____ have soft bodies, use the shells of other animals for protection. _____ they find an empty shell, they climb right into it _____ drag it around with them. _____ the shell doesn't grow with them, they go through several of these 'mobile homes' in a lifetime.

There is strong competition for shells among hermit crabs. _____ they see a crab with what they think is a better shell, a few of them will cooperate to pull the shell away. Then they turn on each other and the one who comes out on top gets the shell!

Hermit crabs make great pets, _____ people don't always know how to look after them. Crabs are often kept in enclosures which are too small _____ are made from unsuitable materials. Glass tanks with a secure screen cover are the best form of housing.

Let's have fun!

Unravel the words and punctuation in each bubble to make a sentence that describes one of the animals in the pictures. Write the sentence next to the correct picture. State whether you have made a **simple**, **compound** or **complex sentence**. The first one has been done for you.

- sharp . me quills , from protect predators my , are very which

- and slowly I very have move . I shell a hard

- like a I'm , I mammal a but fish . really look

- extinct ago I millions of . became years

I have a hard shell and I move very slowly.   _compound_

Unit 12: Animals with armour

Let's have a test!

1 Which sentence has been written correctly?

- ○ A rhino beetle is large, or a rhino is larger.
- ○ A rhino beetle is large, but a rhino is larger.
- ○ A rhino beetle is large, so a rhino is larger.
- ○ A rhino beetle is large, nor a rhino is larger.

In questions 2–6, which word completes the sentence correctly?

2 The fisherman catches lobsters, _____ he has never eaten one.
- ○ so
- ○ yet
- ○ or
- ○ nor

3 The crab was angry _____ it nipped me.
- ○ and
- ○ yet
- ○ but
- ○ or

4 I don't like crabs, _____ do I like lobsters.
- ○ but
- ○ yet
- ○ and
- ○ nor

5 The boy _____ lives next door has a pet turtle.
- ○ which
- ○ whom
- ○ who
- ○ whose

6 I won't show you my pet python, _____ you really want to see it.
- ○ unless
- ○ until
- ○ because
- ○ while

7 Which word can be left out of this sentence without changing its meaning?

I told him that he could have one of my pet lizards.
- ○ that
- ○ could
- ○ of
- ○ my

8 Which sentence combines the information in these three sentences correctly?

The rhino is a large animal. I saw the rhino at the zoo. The rhino has a thick skin.

- ○ The rhino at the zoo has a large, thick skin.
- ○ The rhino has a thick skin which I saw at the zoo.
- ○ The rhino, which I saw at the zoo, is a large animal with a thick skin.
- ○ The rhino, which has a thick skin, is an animal in a large zoo.

Let's write now!

Write an **information report** about an animal with armour. Use **simple**, **compound** and **complex sentences** in your report.

Unit 13 Famous Australians

Focus
Quotation marks and colons; brackets and abbreviations

Oodgeroo Noonuccal

I believe that Oodgeroo Noounuccal was a true hero. She was forced to leave school when she was thirteen, but that did not stop her from following her dream of becoming a writer. In 1964 she became the first Aboriginal poet to publish a book of verse: **'We Are Going'**. It was so popular that it sold out in three days.

More than anything, though, I admire her for her pride in her Aboriginal background and the work she did for her people. In 1970, she established an open-air classroom where people from different backgrounds could learn about Aboriginal culture and society. She also used her poems to encourage all Australians to live together in peace and harmony. In her poem, 'All One Race', she wrote that we are 'All one family'.

Oodgeroo also wrote four books for children: 'Father Sky and Mother Earth', 'Stradbroke Dreamtime', 'Little Fella' and 'The Rainbow Serpent'. In 1985 she appeared in a film: 'The Fringe Dwellers'. This talented Australian is truly a national treasure.

by Gina

This is a personal **response**. A personal response is a person's reaction to a subject or event. Gina uses **quotation marks** around the titles of books, poems and films, and **colons** to show that more information is to follow while expressing her admiration for the poet, Oodgeroo Noonuccal.

Rule!

Quotation marks are used around the titles of books, poems, films, plays, songs, newspapers and magazines; for example, **'We Are Going'** is the title of one of Oodgeroo's books.

If there is a punctuation mark after the title, it comes <u>after</u> the quotation mark; for example, **'We Are Going'.**

Colons (:) are used to show that more information is to follow; for example, the colon after **Oodgeroo also wrote four books for children** shows that the names of the books are to follow.

 ## Let's find them!

Tip!
In printed text, you can use italics instead of quotation marks when writing titles.

Find these titles in the text. Remember to include the **quotation marks**. Write the title of one of Oodgeroo's poems:

 _____

Unit 13: Famous Australians

73

Write the titles of four of Oodgeroo's books.

2 _____   4 _____

3 _____   5 _____

Write the title of the film Oodgeroo appeared in.

6 _____

> **Tip!**
> All the words in the titles of books, poems etc. start with a capital letter. The exceptions are little words like **a**, **an**, **the**, **and**, **of** and **for** (except if they come at the beginning of the title).

Let's go to the next step!

Underline the **punctuation** mistakes in these sentences and write the corrections in the spaces.

For example: Oodgeroo Noonuccal wrote a book of short stories called 'Stradbroke Dreamtime.'   _Dreamtime'._

1 Henry Lawson wrote the poem 'Ballad of The Drover'. _____

2 Banjo Patterson wrote the words for 'Waltzing Matilda.' _____

3 One of my favourite movies is 'the Man from Snowy River'. _____

4 I read the 'Sydney morning Herald' and 'The Australian'. _____

5 Kylie Minogue once starred in the TV show 'Neighbours.' _____

6 The book contains information on many famous Australians. Victor Chang, Cathy Freeman and Ian Thorpe. _____

7 Geoffrey Rush has starred in some famous films. 'Pirates of the Caribbean', 'The King's Speech' and 'Shakespeare in Love'. _____

Let's aim high now!

Fill in the missing **quotation marks** and **colons** in these sentences.

1 The documentary, A Very Short War, is about a famous Australian pilot.

2 Dorothea McKellar wrote a famous poem about Australia called My Country.

3 The conservationist, Ian Kiernan, has co-authored a book called Coming Clean.

4 John Marsden's book, Tomorrow, When the War Began, has been made into a film.

5 Australia's national anthem, Advance Australia Fair, was composed by Peter Dodds McCormick.

6 These are my favourite books by John Marsden Tomorrow When the War Began and The Other Side of Dawn.

7 These are my three favourite poems by Oodgeroo Muncipal Gum, Understand Old One and We Are Going.

Fred Hollows

Fred Hollows **(1929–1993)** was an eye doctor (ophthalmologist) who helped thousands of people in poor countries regain their sight. Born in New Zealand, Hollows did much of his training in the UK. He moved to Australia in 1965 to take up a teaching post at **UNSW** in Sydney and became an Australian citizen in 1989.

Shortly after arriving in Australia, Hollows started working with the Gurindji people in NT and with Aboriginal communities in isolated areas of NSW. Later he started helping those in need in other countries as well, mainly in Africa and Asia. Australians donated generously to help him build an eye lens factory in Eritrea (a country in north-west Africa).

Unfortunately, Fred Hollows didn't live to see all of his dreams come true. He was diagnosed with cancer in 1989 and died four years later. But thanks to the Fred Hollows Foundation (established in 1992), other people are continuing his good work.

by Nick

This is a **biography**. A biography is an account of someone's life written by someone else. Nick uses **brackets** around numbers and words that give additional information about the text, and **abbreviations** to shorten words while telling about the life and work of Fred Hollows.

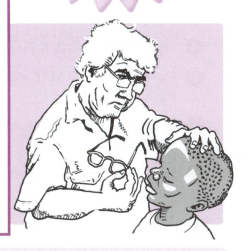

Rule!

Brackets are used around additional information in a sentence; for example, in the first sentence, the dates **(1929–1993)** are placed between brackets because they give more information about Fred Hollows's life.

Abbreviations are the shortened forms of words or groups of words. We use them to save us writing out the whole word all the time; for example, **UNSW** is the abbreviation for **University of New South Wales**.

Let's find them!

Tip! Commas can usually be used in place of brackets.

Find the extra information that has been added about

1. what an eye doctor is called _____
2. where Eritrea is situated _____
3. when the Fred Hollows Foundation was established _____

Find the **abbreviation** of

4. United Kingdom _____
5. Northern Territory _____

Unit 13: **Famous Australians**

6 New South Wales _____

Find the name of the country for which NZ is an **abbreviation**.

7 _____

Let's go to the next step!

Fill in the missing **brackets** in these sentences.

1 Oodgeroo Noonuccal 1920–1993 is a famous Australian poet.

2 Banjo Paterson lived on a property of 40 000 acres 160 km² near Yass.

3 Sir Donald George Bradman The Don had a test batting average of 99.94 runs.

4 Fred Hollows born in New Zealand did most of his work in Australia, Africa and Asia.

5 Dawn Fraser AO MBE was the first woman to swim 100 m freestyle in under a minute.

6 Doctor Victor Chang born Chang Yam Him was a pioneer of heart transplantation in Australia.

7 Nobel Prize winner Howard Florey 1898–1968 studied medicine at the University of Adelaide.

Let's aim high now!

Underline the word or words in these sentences that can be replaced by an **abbreviation** from the box. Write the abbreviation in the space at the end of the sentence.
For example: Edmund Barton, Australia's first prime minister, died in 1920. ___PM___

ACT	Qld	LA	ANZAC	pm	WA	VC

1 Some Australian actors live in Los Angeles in California. _____

2 Hugh Jackman was born in Perth, the capital of Western Australia. _____

3 A number of Australians have received the Victoria Cross for bravery. _____

4 The governor-general is making an important announcement at 4 o'clock. _____

5 The prime minister's official residence is in the Australian Capital Territory. _____

6 Many Australian and New Zealand Army Corps soldiers died at Gallipoli in 1915. _____

7 Neville Bonner, Australia's first Aboriginal senator, died in Ipswich in Queensland in 1999. _____

Let's put it together now!

This student has left out two sets of **brackets**, a **colon** and three lots of **quotation marks** in this biography of Dame Joan Sutherland. She has also written an **abbreviation** incorrectly. Use a red pen to make the corrections for her.

Dame Joan Sutherland 1926–2010 was born in Sydney and went on to become one of the greatest opera singers in the world. She had a strong voice and got a lucky break when she won free singing lessons at the age of nineteen. Her dream was to become an opera star, and in 1951 she went to the uk, where she met and married the Australian pianist, Richard Bonynge pronounced Boning. Among the many famous operas in which she sang the female lead were the following The Magic Flute, Suor Angelica and Hamlet. She retired in 1990.

Let's have fun!

The information that follows the colon in each of these sentences is in the box. Complete each sentence with the correct information.

> Liesel Jones, Lleyton Hewitt and Cadel Evans
> Julia Gillard, Kevin Rudd and John Howard
> Cate Blanchett, Russell Crowe and Hugh Jackman

1. These are my favourite Australian actors: _____

2. These Australian sportsmen and women have achieved great things:
   _____

3. These people have all been prime ministers of Australia: _____

Complete these sentences with the correct information in the box.

> (1897–1935)   (nicknamed the Thorpedo)   (published in 2001)

4. Ian Thorpe _____ won many gold medals for Australia in the swimming pool.

5. Charles Kingsford Smith _____ was a famous Australian aviator who died more than seventy-five years ago.

6. One of my favourite Andy Griffiths books _____ is 'The Day My Bum Went Psycho'.

Complete the addresses on these envelopes with an abbreviation from the box.

> Ave
> Tas
> PO

7. Future Australian Scientist
   2021 Ocean Drive
   Hobart _____
   7000

8. Future Australian Politician
   49 Waratah _____
   Hamilton
   Victoria
   3300

9. Future Australian Swimmer
   _____ Box 5829
   Stirling
   South Australia
   5152

Unit 13: **Famous Australians**   77

Let's have a test!

1 Which sentence has been punctuated correctly?
- ○ Donald Bradman wrote a book called 'My Cricketing Life.'
- ○ Donald Bradman wrote a book called 'My cricketing life'.
- ○ Donald Bradman wrote a book called 'My Cricketing Life'.
- ○ Donald Bradman wrote a book called 'my cricketing life'.

In questions 2–3, where should the quotation marks go in each sentence?

2 This week the TV program An Australian Story is about a famous actor.

3 My favourite poem by Henry Lawson is The Ballad of the Drover.

4 Where should the colon go in this sentence?

These men are Australian authors Patrick White and John Marsden.

5 Which option should be in brackets?

In 2008, Quentin Bryce, born in 1942, became Governor-General of Australia.

6 Which letters or words in this sentence should be in brackets?

The United Nations Environment Program UNEP gave its support to Ian Kiernan's Clean Up the World campaign.
- ○ United Nations
- ○ Environment Program
- ○ UNEP
- ○ Clean Up the World

In questions 7–8, which option is the correct abbreviation for the underlined words?

7 I sent our swimmers a <u>short messaging service</u> to wish them luck.
- ○ SHS ○ SMS ○ SME ○ SES

8 It's Australia <u>versus</u> England in the final of the World Cricket Championships.
- ○ v ○ ver ○ vr ○ vs

Let's write now!

Look in books or on the Internet for information about a famous Australian that you admire. Write a personal **response** to that person's achievements, or a **biography** of the person. Try to use at least one set of **quotation marks**, one set of **brackets**, a **colon** and an **abbreviation** in your writing.

Unit 14 Acting it out

Focus
Adjectival and adverbial clauses and commas; colons, brackets and ellipses

Sadako and the Thousand Cranes

Last week our class went to the theatre to see *Sadako and the Thousand Cranes*. The play is based on Eleanor Coerr's book, **which was published in 1977. Although we had read the book in class**, seeing it come to life on the stage gave me a better understanding of how war affects ordinary people.

The actor who played the part of Sadako portrayed the young girl's liveliness and determination perfectly. She was well supported by the rest of the cast, who all brought something special to their roles. I especially enjoyed the performance of Sadako's brother, whose antics were often hilarious! The audience laughed **whenever he came on stage. I was also fascinated by the sets, which unfolded like giant origami designs.**

Sadako's story is important because it carries such a strong message about the horrors of war. It is even more powerful when it is acted out on the stage.

by Tori

This is a **review**. A review is a personal reaction to a book or show. Tori uses **adjectival clauses** to give more information about nouns and **adverbial clauses** to give more information about verbs while expressing her opinion about the play, *Sadako and the Thousand Cranes*. She sometimes uses **commas** to separate the clauses from the rest of the sentence, making the text easier to understand.

Rule!

Adjectival clauses are dependent clauses that
- give more information about nouns.
- are usually introduced by the relative pronouns *who*, *whose*, *whom*, *which* or *that*; for example, **which was published in 1977** gives more information about Eleanor Coerr's book.

Adverbial clauses are dependent clauses that
- give more information about verbs; for example, **whenever he came on stage** gives more information about when the audience laughed.
- are usually introduced by a conjunction; for example, **Although we had read the book in class**.

These are some of the conjunctions that introduce dependent clauses: **after**, **although**, **as**, **because**, **before**, **if**, **once**, **since**, **though**, **unless**, **until**, **when**, **whenever**, **whereas**, **whether** and **while**.

Commas are sometimes used to separate clauses from the rest of the sentence to make the text easier to understand; for example, **I was also fascinated by the sets, which unfolded like giant origami designs.**

Let's find them!

Find three **relative pronouns** that introduce **adjectival clauses** in the text.

1) _____ 2) _____ 3) _____

Find four **conjunctions** that introduce **adverbial clauses** in the text.

4) _____ 5) _____ 6) _____ 7) _____

> **Tip!**
> Remember: an **adjectival clause** is introduced by a **relative pronoun** and an **adverbial clause** by a **conjunction**.

Let's go to the next step!

Fill in the missing **commas** in these sentences.

1) Once the curtain went up the actor started to relax.
2) The play which recently won an award was very funny.
3) Before I go on stage I always have butterflies in my tummy.
4) The actors who had been rehearsing all day were exhausted.
5) Although I enjoy watching plays I would rather go to the movies.
6) When you go to the theatre make sure you have your ticket with you!
7) The director whose parents had been famous actors was trying to make a name for himself.

Let's aim high now!

Complete each sentence with a clause from the box. State whether it is an **adjectival clause** or an **adverbial clause**. For example, The play, <u>which is due to open next week</u>, is set in the 1970s. _____*adjectival*_____

> who is still very young
> since I went with the school last year
> whose latest play is due to open soon
> if this one is a success
>
> because we arrived late
> which I have yet to see
> after I had read the book

1) She will write another play _____. _____
2) I watched the play _____. _____
3) We missed the first act _____. _____
4) The actor, _____, is playing the part of an old man. _____
5) The playwright, _____, is very nervous. _____
6) The play, _____, has received excellent reviews. _____
7) I haven't been to the theatre _____. _____

The Word Market

Stallholder: (turning to Melissa) And what about you, young lady? What's your problem?

Melissa: **Well … oh, I know!** Whenever I say something, everyone always says "Nonsense!"

Stallholder: Mmm … that's a shame. But never mind, I've got just the thing for you —a good dollop of sense (hands her the card marked 'sense'). Take some of this before bedtime each night and nobody will ever accuse you of talking nonsense again.

Melissa: (looking uncertain) Are you sure it will work?

Stallholder: Of course it will … trust me. (Turns to Lenny) And what about you, young man? Why don't you do well at school?

by Hyun

This is part of a **script** for a play. A script contains the dialogue and stage directions for the actors and other people involved in a play to follow. Hyun uses **colons** after the speakers' names, **brackets** around stage directions and **ellipses** to show pauses in speech in this part of his script.

In Unit 13 you learnt that **colons** (:) are used to show that more information is to follow. Colons are also used after the speaker's name in a script or interview; for example, **Stallholder:**

You also learnt in Unit 13 that **brackets** are used around additional information in a sentence. Brackets are also used around stage directions in scripts; for example, **(turning to Melissa)** tells the actor what he should be doing.

Ellipses (singular: ellipsis) consist of three dots (**…**). They show a pause in speech; for example, **Well … oh, I know!**

Let's find them!

Underline the words in **brackets**, put a circle around the **colons** and put boxes around the **ellipses** in these phrases and sentences from the script.

1. Stallholder: Mmm … that's a shame.
2. a good dollop of sense (hands her the card marked 'sense')

Unit 14: **Acting it out**

3. Melissa: (looking uncertain)

4. Stallholder: Of course it will … trust me. (Turns to Lenny)

Let's go to the next step!

Some of the **brackets**, **colons** and **ellipses** in these lines from a script are in the wrong place. Use a red pen to show where they should be.
For example: Lenny (looking puzzled) I think it's because: I keep falling asleep in class.

1. Rich lady (to stallholder) Oh dear: oh dear.

2. Father: smacking his lips (This is truly scrumptious!)

3. Fairies Thank you, Sir: Can we pay you in fairy dust?

4. Ballerina: falling over her feet (Look how clumsy I am!)

5. Stallholder: Let me think ah yes, this is … the card for you!

6. Athlete: (I've got a big race tomorrow.) Moves towards the Athletes' Stall.

7. Stallholder: … Mmmm let's see if I have something to make you dainty again.

Let's aim high now!

Fill in the missing **brackets**, **colons** and **ellipses** in these lines from a script.

1. Shopkeeper: turning to customer Will that be all, Madam?

2. Crier: moving to centre stage Words for sale! Words for sale!

3. Melissa: (shouting from her room) Mum, where's oh, never mind.

4. Customer (taking out her wallet) Yes, that's all for now, thank you.

5. Lady: (looking surprised) What on I don't believe it! My wallet is empty!

6. Twinkletoes (walking towards Fairy Stall) I wonder what we'll find here?

7. Fairy: Oh, that's much better. Starts dancing about I can dance again!

Let's put it together now!

This student has left out some important punctuation marks in this section of his script. Use a red pen to fill in the missing **commas**, **colons**, **brackets** and **ellipses**. There are seven mistakes altogether.

Goblin #1: turning to the other goblins Have you noticed that I haven't been as mean as usual lately?

Goblin #2 Now that you mention it I haven't felt like annoying anyone all week.

Goblin #3 looking thoughtful Mmmm now that's interesting. I haven't been nearly as horrible as I normally am.

Goblin #1: If you ask me it's high time we did something about it!

Let's have fun!

Two of the lines from the script of this play have started floating around the stage. See if you can put them back together again. Make sure you use all of the **punctuation marks**!

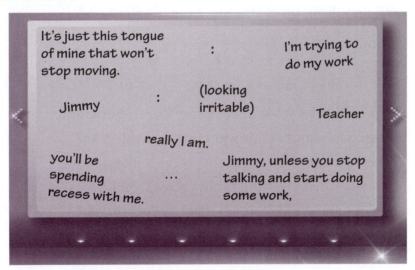

Write the lines out correctly below.

_____   _____
_____   _____
_____   _____
_____   _____
_____   _____
_____   _____

Unit 14: **Acting it out**   83

Let's have a test!

In questions 1–2, which word completes the sentence correctly?

1 The actor, _____ father is a director, is auditioning for the part.
○ who   ○ that   ○ which   ○ whose

2 I will give the role of the wicked witch to Tessa, _____ you want it.
○ if   ○ unless   ○ until   ○ because

In questions 3–4, which word and punctuation completes the sentence correctly?

3 The role of the prince _____ is the one he wants, has been taken.
○ , which   ○ which,   ○ , who   ○ who,

4 I will audition for the part _____ I don't think I'll get it.
○ , if   ○ if,   ○ , although   ○ although,

5 Where should the brackets go in this line from a script?

Doctor: Take some of this hands her the medicine and you'll soon feel better.

6 Where should the ellipsis go in this line from a script?

Lady: (scratching around in her bag) Now where oh, here it is!

In questions 7–8, which lines from a script have been punctuated correctly?

7 ○ Peter: moving forward) Is this what you're looking for?
○ Peter (moving forward) Is this what you're looking for?
○ Peter: (moving forward) Is this what you're looking for?
○ Peter: (moving forward Is this what you're looking for?

8 ○ Zoe: (looking confused) But … No! I don't believe it!
○ Zoe: looking confused … But no! I don't believe it!
○ Zoe … (looking confused) But no: I don't believe it!
○ Zoe: (looking confused) … But no I don't believe it!

Let's write now!

Choose one of the following.

1. Write a **review** of a play you have watched. Use **adjectival** and **adverbial clauses** in your review.
2. Write a **script** for a scene from a play. Use **colons**, **brackets** and **ellipses** to punctuate the lines.

Unit 15 Changing fashions

Focus
Apostrophes that show contraction; apostrophes that show ownership

Edward's diary

30th November 1688

Today I got some very exciting news: **I'm** to accompany Papa the next time he goes to see the king! Papa says I'll need a new outfit. He's going to take me to his tailor, who'll take my measurements and make me a pair of breeches, a ruffled long-sleeved shirt, a silk vest and a velvet coat. Papa's also ordered some new stockings for me and I'm getting a pair of square-toed shoes all decorated with ribbons and bows! Best of all, though, I'll be getting my first wig! Papa says my outfit wouldn't be complete without one. I've already chosen the one I want. It's got a centre part and the curls will flow down my shoulders and back. I'm going to look ever so grand!

This is a **diary entry**. A diary entry is a record people keep of things that are happening or have happened to them. Edward uses **apostrophes** in place of missing letters to shorten words and make them easier to say while telling about his new outfit.

Contractions
- are formed when two words are joined to make one, shorter word; for example, **I'm** is short for **I am**.
- have **apostrophes** (') in place of the missing letters; for example, in *I'm*, the apostrophe takes the place of the *a* in *am*.

Rule! Watch out for these tricky words:
- It's hard to say 'willn't' for **will not**, so we say **won't**.
- We use **its** without the apostrophe when it's a possessive pronoun; for example, **The hat has lost its shape.**
- The word **who's** is short for **who is**, while **whose** means 'who it belongs to'; for example, **The man who's wearing a wig/the man whose wig it is.**

Unit 15: Changing fashions   85

Let's find them!

Find these **contractions** in the text.

1. I will _____
2. he is _____
3. who will _____
4. Papa has _____
5. would not _____
6. I have _____
7. it has _____
8. I am _____

Let's go to the next step!

Use a red pen to fill in the missing **apostrophes** in the **contractions** in these sentences.

1. I dont think Id have liked wearing a curly wig.
2. She doesnt know what people wore a hundred years ago.
3. I wanted to try on the old breeches, but they wouldnt let me.
4. Theyre going to buy him a new outfit thats more fashionable.
5. I havent seen the movie, but I believe the costumes are magnificent.
6. He didnt want to wear the fancy hat, but his sister said itd make him look cool.
7. We arent going to the dress-up party because we wont be here that weekend.

Let's aim high now!

Tip!
Be careful! Some sentences have two sets of words that can be written as **contractions**.

Underline the words that can be joined to make one word, or that can be shortened, and then write the **contractions** in the spaces.

1. Who is going to try on this hat? _____
2. This jacket does not go with that outfit. _____
3. You must not wear dull colours if they do not suit you. _____
4. My mother is going to make me an outfit for the party. _____
5. You should have worn your other shoes with that dress. _____
6. My sister is upset because she cannot find her favourite bag. _____
7. We have told him not to wear those jeans, but he will not listen. _____

Weird fashions

Men's, women's and children's fashions have gone through many changes during the last 6000 years. Some fashions have been sensible and smart, but others have been downright weird! In Venice in the 16th and 17th centuries, **a rich lady's wardrobe** would include at least one pair of *chopines*—shoes with heels of cork or wood that were between 17 and 50 cm high! These ladies often needed a servant's help to walk. Even today, **ladies' shoes** can be up to 18 cm high, which, according to doctors' reports, can result in knee and joint problems.

Other weird fashions from the past include wearing false eyelashes made from a mouse's skin, **women's feet** being bound to prevent them from growing too big and little boys being dressed in girls' clothes. Who knows what society's next idea of what looks cool will be!

by Narelle

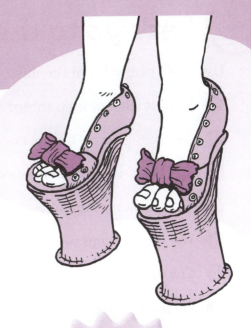

This is a **description**. Remember: a description creates a mind picture of a person, place, object or event. Narelle uses **apostrophes** to show ownership while describing weird fashions from the past.

Apostrophes are also used to show ownership; for example, **a rich lady's wardrobe**. The apostrophe shows that the wardrobe **belongs to** the rich lady.

 Rule!
- If there is one owner, the apostrophe comes before the *s*; for example, **lady's wardrobe**.
- If there is more than one owner, the apostrophe comes after the *s*; for example, **ladies' shoes**.
- For irregular plurals such as **women**, the apostrophe always comes before the *s*; for example, **women's feet**.

 ## Let's find them!

Tip! Normal plurals do not have apostrophes because they don't own anything; for example, These <u>ladies</u> often needed help to walk.

According to the text, what do these people or things **own**?

1. men _____
2. children _____
3. servant _____
4. doctors _____
5. mouse _____
6. girls _____
7. society _____

Unit 15: **Changing fashions**   87

Let's go to the next step!

Use a red pen to fill in the missing **apostrophes** in these sentences.

1. Wool is made from a sheep's fleece.
2. One of the glove's fingers had a hole in it.
3. The king's new garment was made from the finest wool.
4. The people's fashionable clothes were destroyed in the fire.
5. The dress's hems were decorated with beads and sequins.
6. Crocodiles' skins were once made into expensive handbags.
7. My friend's mother is going to buy her a new dress for her birthday.

Let's aim high now!

Underline the phrases that show possession and then rewrite them with an **apostrophe**. Write out the whole sentence.

For example: The <u>name of the manufacturer</u> appears on the label.
The manufacturer's name appears on the label.

1. The bodice of the dress is made of satin.

2. The outfits of Lady Gaga are often outrageous.

3. The costumes of the singers were very colourful.

4. The buttons of the garment are shaped like pearls.

5. The clothes of the teachers are very old-fashioned.

6. The hair of the new student has been cut in the latest style.

7. You can buy the collections of the designers at the new store.

Let's put it together now!

This student has left out all of the **apostrophes** in this part of her diary entry. Use a red pen to fill them in for her.

24th March 1999

I cant believe it! My brothers latest thing is to wear his pants so that most of his undies are showing! He thinks its cool. I dont. Mums pleas and Dads harsh words have fallen on deaf ears. Today he wanted me to go to the shops with him. I told him Id rather eat worms.

Let's have fun!

Fit the **contractions** of the pairs of words in the box into the spaces. The number of spaces and the position of the **apostrophes** are your clues. The first one has been done for you.

| he would | you are | I would | they are |
| you would | might not | fashion is | we are |

1. h e ' d
2. ☐☐☐ ' ☐☐
3. ☐ ' ☐
4. ☐☐☐☐☐☐☐ ' ☐
5. ☐☐ ' ☐☐
6. ☐☐☐☐☐☐☐ ' ☐
7. ☐☐☐☐ ' ☐☐
8. ☐☐☐ ' ☐

Now fill the words that complete these sentences into the correct space below. The position of the **apostrophe** is your clue in each case.

9. These shoes belong to the boy.
   They are the _____ shoes.

10. Those gloves belong to the children.
    They are the _____ gloves.

11. This scarf belongs to the woman.
    It is the _____ scarf.

12. These caps belong to the athletes.
    They are the _____ caps.

13. Those coats belonged to the princes.
    They are the _____ coats.

Unit 15: Changing fashions 89

Let's have a test!

1. Which sentence has been punctuated correctly?

- ○ Moira is'nt wearing her new outfit.
- ○ Moira isn't wearing her new outfit.
- ○ Moira isnt' wearing her new outfit.
- ○ Moira i'snt wearing her new outfit.

In questions 2–4, which pair of words completes the sentence correctly?

2. _____ leave when _____ found their coats.
- ○ You've, you'll
- ○ He's, he'll
- ○ They'll, they've
- ○ They've, they'll

3. I _____ worn my new suit, but _____ at the dry cleaners.
- ○ would've, it's
- ○ could've, they're
- ○ would've, its
- ○ should've, its

4. These _____ hats are on sale in most _____.
- ○ childrens', stores
- ○ children's, store's
- ○ children's, stores'
- ○ children's, stores

5. Which underlined words can be replaced with *won't*?
- ○ They <u>were not</u> wearing their best clothes.
- ○ <u>We were</u> wearing our best clothes.
- ○ <u>Were we</u> supposed to wear our best clothes?
- ○ We <u>will not</u> wear our best clothes.

In questions 6–7, which sentence has been punctuated correctly?

6.
- ○ The dresse's hem has come loose.
- ○ The dresses' hem has come loose.
- ○ The dress's hem has come loose.
- ○ The dress'es hem has come loose.

7.
- ○ I found this shirt in the men's department.
- ○ I found this shirt in the mens' department.
- ○ I found this shirt in the ladys' department.
- ○ I found this shirt in the ladie's department.

8. Which word completes this sentence correctly?

The _____ new outfit is very cute.
- ○ babies'
- ○ babys'
- ○ babie's
- ○ baby's

Let's write now!

Look in books or on the Internet for information about unusual fashions, either from the past or in the present day. Write a **description** of the one you have chosen. Use **apostrophes** to show where letters have been left out in **contractions** and to show ownership.

Unit 16: Rules and regulations

✪ Focus
Modality and adverbs; nominalisation

Why we need school rules

Some people may think that many of our school rules are unnecessary, but I think we **must** have them! If we didn't have playground rules, for example, it **could** result in some serious accidents at recess and lunch break. Also, if students didn't have to get a late note from the office, they might start coming to school halfway through the day!

Perhaps there are some schools that have silly rules, like giving extra homework for talking in class, but I believe that the rules at our school are pretty sensible. Thank goodness we're not allowed to push and shove each other. I **definitely** would not like to end up at the bottom of the stairs with a broken arm, or **maybe** worse!

We must have school rules. Without them, our school would be chaotic!

by Leila

This is an **exposition**. An exposition expresses and gives reasons for an opinion, usually in order to convince others. Leila uses **modal verbs** and **adverbs** to show how certain she is of the need for school rules.

Modal verbs are auxiliary verbs that show how certain we are about something. This is called **modality**.

Auxiliary verbs that show certainty have **high modality**; for example: **must**, **must not**, **will**, **will not**.

Auxiliary verbs that show uncertainty have **low modality**; for example: **might**, **might not**, **could**, **could not**.

Adverbs can also have modality. Adverbs that show high modality include words like **definitely**, **certainly** and **always**. Adverbs that show low modality include words like **perhaps**, **maybe** and **sometimes**.

Let's find them!

Find these auxiliary verbs and adverbs in the text and write down whether they show **high** or **low modality**.

1 may _____

2. certainly _____

3. could _____

4. might _____

5. perhaps _____

6. definitely _____

7. must _____

Let's go to the next step!

Underline the **modal verb** or **adverb** in each of these sentences and state whether it expresses certainty or uncertainty.

For example: I might read that set of rules later. _____uncertainty_____

1. We could get rid of that rule. _____

2. I will not break that rule again! _____

3. That boy always disobeys the rules. _____

4. You must stop if the traffic light is red. _____

5. He probably didn't see the 'No Parking' sign. _____

6. We may not tell those people about the new rule. _____

7. I definitely don't want to be punished for breaking the law. _____

Let's aim high now!

Complete these sentences by choosing the correct **verb** or **adverb** in brackets. The instruction at the end of the sentence will help you choose the correct word. Cross out the one that is wrong.

For example: I (might/will) pay my parking fine. (certainty)

1. They (may/will) change some of these rules. (uncertainty)

2. He (will not/might not) be sent off for that illegal tackle. (uncertainty)

3. They (could/must) pass a law to protect that bushland. (certainty)

4. You (must not/should not) feed the animals in the reserve. (certainty)

5. (Perhaps/Surely) there are some rules that can be broken. (uncertainty)

6. That is (positively/possibly) the silliest rule I've ever heard of. (certainty)

7. She is (probably/definitely) the most disobedient girl in the school. (certainty)

The purpose of rules and regulations in society

The main purpose of the rules and regulations in our society is to give it organisation and structure. Rules that carry **punishments** if they are broken are mainly made by governments. Many of these rules are for our protection, but they also make us take responsibility for our behaviour. Fortunately, in our society most people recognise the importance of rules and tend to respect them. They understand, for example, that without traffic rules there would be confusion on the roads and people's safety would be at risk.

We might not always like our rules and regulations, but no society can function smoothly without them.

by Simon

This is another **exposition**. Simon uses **nominalised** words to express concepts and ideas and to make his writing sound more formal while convincing us of the need for rules and regulations.

Verbs and adjectives can be turned into nouns, usually by adding suffixes. This is called **nominalisation**; for example, the noun **punishments** is formed from the verb *punish*.

Let's find them!

Find these **nominalised** words in the text.

1. the verb *organise* _____
2. the verb *protect* _____
3. the adjective *responsible* _____
4. the verb *behave* _____
5. the adjective *important* _____
6. the verb *confuse* _____
7. the adjective *safe* _____

Tip!

Nominalised words are abstract nouns. They make our speech and writing sound more formal.

Unit 16: **Rules and regulations**

Let's go to the next step!

Tip! Use a dictionary to check your spelling!

Choose a suffix to **nominalise** each verb or adjective below. Write the new word in the correct column.
The first one has been done for you.

	Verb/adjective	ion	ity	ance	ness
1	describe	description			
2	secure				
3	populate				
4	childish				
5	enter				
6	forgetful				
7	fatal				
8	resist				
9	explode				
10	visible				
11	insure				
12	friendly				
13	interrupt				
14	accept				

Let's aim high now!

Complete these sentences by **nominalising** the verbs and adjectives in brackets (turn them into nouns).

For example: They have every (intend) _____intention_____ of passing that law.

1. Police officers perform an important (serve) _____ in society.

2. We have received a lot of (inform) _____ about the new law.

3. Police officers are responsible for the (enforce) _____ of the law.

4. The politician mentioned the new law in a (state) _____ to the press.

5. You could receive a fine if you do not follow the correct (proceed) _____.

6. They need the (approve) _____ of the community before they can pass that law.

7. The purpose of the new law is to reduce the amount of (pollute) _____ in the atmosphere.

94   Year 6 Grammar and Punctuation Workbook

Let's put it together now!

The teacher has made a ^ sign to show this student where he should have used a **modal verb** or **adverb** and he has underlined the words that need to be **nominalised**. Use a red pen to make the corrections.
The missing modals are *might*, *definitely* and *could*.

The council wants to make our local park a dog-friendly area, where dogs no longer have to be leashed. I am ^ against this idea. It will place both the dogs and the people who use the park in <u>dangerous</u>. Some dogs ^ run off and end up on a busy road, or they ^ hurt a young child. Parks are for people. They are for <u>recreate</u> and <u>relax</u>. People don't want to be bothered by strange animals sniffing around their picnic lunch, or interfering with their games. I am happy to share the park with dogs, as long as they are on a leash. Come on, Councillors! Where is your sense of <u>responsible</u>?

Let's have fun!

Nominalise these verbs (turn them into nouns) and then circle the letter indicated by the number. The circled letters spell a rule that you often hear at school. Write the rule in the space below. Use a dictionary if necessary.

Verb	Noun		Letter
prepare	_____	(11th)	_____
revise	_____	(7th)	_____
refuse	_____	(3rd)	_____
see	_____	(2nd)	_____
agree	_____	(2nd)	_____
think	_____	(6th)	_____
create	_____	(5th)	_____
believe	_____	(4th)	_____
decide	_____	(8th)	_____
judge	_____	(4th)	_____

Rule: _____

Unit 16: **Rules and regulations**

Let's have a test!

In questions 1–2, which sentence expresses certainty?

1. ◯ He might have broken the law.   ◯ He may have broken the law.
   ◯ He could have broken the law.   ◯ He must have broken the law.

2. ◯ He will probably get a fine.   ◯ Perhaps he will get a fine.
   ◯ He will definitely get a fine.   ◯ Maybe he will get a fine.

In questions 3–4, which sentence expresses uncertainty?

3. ◯ They will make it a rule.   ◯ They might make it a rule.
   ◯ They will not make it a rule.   ◯ They must not make it a rule.

4. ◯ I always obey the rules.   ◯ I never obey the rules.
   ◯ I sometimes obey the rules.   ◯ I certainly obey the rules.

In questions 5–6, which word completes the sentence correctly?

5. Breaking the law could result in _____.
   ◯ imprison   ◯ imprisoned
   ◯ imprisons   ◯ imprisonment

6. The _____ of the police officer prevented a crime.
   ◯ alert   ◯ alertness
   ◯ alerted   ◯ alertly

7. In which sentence is the underlined word a noun?
   ◯ The jury has come to a decision.
   ◯ The jury has decided.
   ◯ The jury is still deciding.
   ◯ The jury decides if she is guilty.

8. Which suffix will turn the underlined word into a noun?

   The establish of a police force brought peace to the region.
   ◯ ness   ◯ ance
   ◯ ity   ◯ ment

Let's write now!

Choose a school rule that you think is either useful or a waste of time. Write an **exposition** in which you argue for or against keeping the rule. Use **modal verbs** and **adverbs** to persuade readers to your point of view, and **nominalised** words to express concepts and ideas.

Unit 17 Television

Focus
Evaluative language; emotive language

Is television a good or bad influence on young people?

Neil and Gina have different opinions about the effects of television on young people. This is what they have to say about it.

Neil: I think that television is one of the most amazing inventions of all time. It's **a brilliant source of entertainment**, and many programs are informative and interesting. Watching TV is enjoyable and relaxing, especially after a tiring day at school. I don't believe that watching television does young people any harm.

Gina: I believe that TV has **a bad effect** on young people. Many of the programs are violent, even those that are shown during prime time, and others are just plain boring. I think that watching too much television numbs our brains and turns us into couch potatoes.

This is part of a **debate**. A debate is a type of discussion in which individuals argue for or against a particular topic. Neil and Gina use **evaluative language** to express their opinions, judgements and points of view on the effect of television on young people.

Evaluative language is language that expresses opinions, judgements or points of view; for example, **a <u>brilliant</u> source of entertainment**, **a <u>bad</u> effect**.

Let's find them!

Tip!
Adjectives are often used to express opinions.

Find eight **adjectives** in the text that express opinions. Don't use the ones in bold.

1. _____
2. _____

Unit 17: Television 97

3 _____   6 _____
4 _____   7 _____
5 _____   8 _____

Let's go to the next step!

Adjectives can express positive or negative opinions. Underline the adjectives that express opinions in these sentences. State whether the opinions are positive or negative.

For example: That is an <u>excellent</u> program! _____ *positive* _____

1. The show has a poor storyline. _____

2. The actors in that TV show are superb. _____

3. Lots of TV programs make for dull viewing. _____

4. The clumsy boy walked right into the TV set. _____

5. The popular politician appears on TV regularly. _____

6. The Johnsons are happy with their new TV set. _____

7. The TV channel provides outstanding entertainment. _____

Let's aim high now!

Underline the **adjectives** in these sentences and state whether the sentence is expressing a fact or an opinion.

> **Tip!**
> Adjectives can express facts as well as opinions. A fact is something we know to be true; for example, **Some television sets are <u>expensive</u>**.

1. Modern television sets have flat screens.
_____

2. Yesterday I watched a funny movie on TV. _____

3. The scenery in the documentary is beautiful. _____

4. The program about dinosaurs was interesting. _____

5. The program is narrated by an Australian actor. _____

6. Some television announcers are young women. _____

7. Wildlife documentaries are more entertaining than reality shows.
_____

How would you like to see these comments on your report card?

She has **polluted** our air with **toxic** fumes.

She has poisoned our waterways with noxious chemicals.

He has hunted defenceless animals to extinction.

He has chopped down ancient forests and destroyed fragile ecosystems.

Sadly, humans are guilty of these crimes against nature. To find out what you can do to improve the comments on our report card, go to www.protectourplanet.net.

This is an **advertisement**. An advertisement persuades people to buy or do things. The advertiser uses **emotive language** to get an emotional reaction from people in order to persuade them to change their behaviour.

Emotive language is language that gets an emotional reaction from people; for example, the words **polluted** and **toxic** make us feel a mixture of anger and disgust.

Emotive language is all around us—in advertisements, news headlines, reports, speeches, interviews and everyday interactions between people. The feelings it creates in us include fear, guilt, sympathy, pity, joy, disgust, anger, respect and sorrow.

Let's find them!

Find these examples of **emotive language** in the text.

1. the adjective that makes us feel pity for animals _____

2. the verb that makes us feel anger at what has been done to our waterways
   _____

3. the adjective that makes us feel disgust for the chemicals in our waterways
   _____

4. the adjective that makes us feel respect for the forests that have been chopped down
   _____

5. the verb that makes us feel anger at what we have done to ecosystems
   _____

6 the adjective that makes us feel sympathy for ecosystems _____

7 the noun that makes us feel guilt at what we have done to nature _____

Let's go to the next step!

Complete these sentences from TV newscasts by underlining the more **emotive** word in brackets.

For example: I (<u>hate</u>/dislike) programs about insects.

1 The local team has (raced/moved) into the lead.

2 House prices have (risen/skyrocketed) this year.

3 The Sting Rays (beat/crushed) the Lions by forty points.

4 Wild winds have (ripped/blown) roofs off buildings in Victoria.

5 A herd of cows (stampeded/ran) through the streets of the town.

6 A (group, mob) of protesters (hurled/threw) bottles at the police.

7 A man in Western Australia has been (attacked/savaged) by a shark.

Let's aim high now!

Find a word in each of these sentences about a TV program that can be replaced with a more **emotive** word from the box. The words must be similar in meaning. Underline the word and write its replacement in the space.

For example: She was <u>surprised</u> to see him. _____*shocked*_____

| exhausted | furious | terrified | overjoyed | hilarious | agony | criminal |

1 The clowns were funny. _____

2 The little girl was frightened. _____

3 The runners were tired after the marathon. _____

4 The man was sentenced to ten years in prison. _____

5 His mother was cross when he came home late. _____

6 The contestant was pleased when she won the big prize. _____

7 The rescue squad found the climber writhing in pain on

the ledge. _____

Let's put it together now!

This student is unsure where to use these **evaluative** and **emotive** words in his argument on the positive effects of TV. Help him put the words in the right places.

> devastating   excellent   risk   alarming   unsuitable   important   fear

I agree that some television programs are _____ for young people. However, there are also lots of _____ shows that give us _____ information. For instance, last night I watched a program about the _____ effects of global warming on the Arctic region. Apparently, the ice is melting at an _____ rate, and experts _____ that the people, wildlife and plants in the area are at _____.

Let's have fun!

Match the TV program in Column B with the comment about it in Column A. Shade the matching pairs the same colour.

> **Tip!**
> Notice the **evaluative** and **emotive** language in the comments!

	Column A	Column B
1	Ambitious young athletes will find this program inspiring.	Cinderella Goes to Hollywood
2	Teens will love this exciting new adventure series.	My Best Friend
3	This is an informative, if somewhat dull, program about the discovery of gold in Australia.	Diary of a Future Champion
4	Not too many people will be enthralled by this new version of a famous fairy tale.	Colour My World
5	Some people might find the images in this new wildlife series distressing.	A Wild Ride!
6	This heart-warming story explores the special relationship between humans and their pets.	The Hunters
7	Join us on this amazing journey into an artist's strange world.	In Search of a Fortune

Unit 17: **Television**

Let's have a test!

1 Which sentence expresses an opinion?
- ◯ They have an old television set.
- ◯ Their television set is small.
- ◯ Their television set has a black frame.
- ◯ Their television set is ugly.

2 Which word in this sentence shows the writer's opinion of television?

Television, which was invented in the twentieth century, is a wonderful form of entertainment.
- ◯ twentieth
- ◯ wonderful
- ◯ form
- ◯ entertainment

3 Which sentence expresses a fact?
- ◯ That program is great.
- ◯ That program is awful.
- ◯ That program is new.
- ◯ That program is boring.

4 Which word completes the second sentence correctly?

I enjoyed watching that program. It was _____.
- ◯ entertaining
- ◯ dull
- ◯ silly
- ◯ confusing

5 Which sentence contains emotive language?
- ◯ Some boys damaged the cameraman's equipment.
- ◯ Vandals wrecked the cameraman's equipment.
- ◯ Someone broke the cameraman's equipment.
- ◯ The cameraman dropped his equipment when he tripped.

In questions 6–8, which is the most emotive word to complete each sentence?

6 The images on the news showed water _____ through the town.
- ◯ flowing
- ◯ trickling
- ◯ surging
- ◯ moving

7 The program is about a boy with _____ manners.
- ◯ bad
- ◯ unusual
- ◯ no
- ◯ revolting

8 The weather report warned that _____ weather was on its way.
- ◯ cold
- ◯ icy
- ◯ cool
- ◯ chilly

Let's write now!

Choose one of the following. Use **evaluative** and **emotive** language.

1. Write a **debate** in which you express your point of view on whether or not television is a bad influence on young people.
2. Create an **advertisement** that persuades people to buy or do something.

Unit 18 Time

Focus
Figures of speech: similes and metaphors; personification

Time poems by Year 6 students

Time is like a freight train that keeps on trundling by.
Time is like the rain, sprinkling minutes from on high.
Time is like a drummer, who never skips a beat.
Time is like a wheel that never stops turning.
by Anthea

Time can be as soft as a dove, gently coaxing the plants to grow.
Time can be as cruel as a tyrant, covering the land with winter snow.
Time can be as quiet as a cat, stealthily approaching on padded paws.
Time can be as loud as thunder, boldly announcing each passing hour.
by Rajit

Time is a factory that churns out minutes and seconds.
Time is a furnace that burns away the days.
Time is a river that carries us on its current.
Time is a disappearing act. Where does it all go?
by Mulin

These are **poems**. Poems are texts that express ideas or describe people and things in imaginative ways. These Year 6 students have used **similes** and **metaphors** to imaginatively compare time to different things.

Figures of speech use words to create visual images and sound effects.

Similes are figures of speech that compare objects or ideas using the words *like* or *as*; for example, **Time is <u>like</u> a freight train**, **Time can be <u>as</u> soft <u>as</u> a dove**.

Metaphors are figures of speech that make comparisons where one thing is said to be something else; for example, **Time <u>is</u> a factory**.

Let's find them!

Find four examples of **similes** and three examples of **metaphors** in the texts and write them in the spaces. Don't use the ones in bold.

 1 _____

Unit 18: Time   103

2 _____   5 _____
3 _____   6 _____
4 _____   7 _____

Let's go to the next step!

Complete the **similes** in these sentences with a word or phrase from the box.

| a ruler | the wind | two sharp needles | a bird |
| the earth | a snail | a feather | |

1 Time rushes by like _____.

2 Time is as old as _____ itself.

3 His new watch is as light as _____.

4 Time seemed to move as slowly as _____.

5 The clock's hands are like _____.

6 Time is like _____, dividing the day into hours and minutes.

7 If I didn't have to worry about time, I'd be as free as _____.

Let's aim high now!

Complete the **metaphors** in these sentences with a word or phrase from the box.

| a gift | money | music | a rollercoaster ride |
| at a donkey's pace | bridge | the slow passage | |

1 For many people in business, time is _____.

2 Time is _____ that we should all use wisely.

3 Time is the _____ between the past and the present.

4 The sound of the clock striking three was _____ to my ears.

5 Life is _____ that everyone has to go on.

6 In that sleepy little town, time moves _____.

7 Mountains are worn away by _____ of time.

Time

Time can march, time can stand still,

Time is something we sometimes kill.

Time can race, time can crawl,

Time can give us a wake-up call.

Time has hands, time has a face,

Time strides ahead at a steady pace.

But there's one thing it seems that time can't do…

When it comes to my homework, it hasn't a clue!

by Nathan

This is another **poem**. Nathan uses **personification** to give time human qualities to make it easier for us to relate to.

Personification is a special type of **metaphor**. It gives objects human qualities, making them easier for us to relate to; for example, **Time can <u>march</u>**.

Let's find them!

Apart from being able to march, find seven things that time can do or that time has that make it seem human. Write the answers in the spaces.

1. _____
2. _____
3. _____
4. _____
5. _____
6. _____
7. _____

Unit 18: **Time**

Let's go to the next step!

Choose the option in brackets that **personifies** the subject in each of these sentences.
For example: Rays of light (peeped/appeared) over the horizon.

1. The hands of the clock (ticked/crept) steadily on.

2. Darkness (covered/embraced) the earth as night fell.

3. The hours (rushed/passed) by in a blur of excitement.

4. The sun shone (angrily/brightly) on the parched earth.

5. The sun (hid/went) behind the clouds in the late afternoon.

6. Today our grandfather clock (forgot to/did not) strike the hours.

7. The sun (shone/smiled) down on the earth as the clock struck noon.

Let's aim high now!

Underline the word or phrase that gives the subject of each sentence a human quality.
For example: The clock held up both hands to signal noon.

Tip!
Sometimes there is more than one word or phrase in the sentence that needs to be underlined.

1. Time won't wait for you, so you'd better hurry up!

2. My alarm clock screams in my ear every morning.

3. The clock announced that it was time for me to leave.

4. The sun wakes up at dawn to rule the world once more.

5. Time gobbles up the minutes, but eats the hours more slowly.

6. The shadows stretched forth their arms as the afternoon wore on.

7. My alarm clock reminds me every morning that I have to go to school.

Let's put it together now!

This student isn't sure how to complete the **similes**, **metaphors** and **personification** in this poem. Help her by placing the words in the correct places.

| is | dancing | bathes | veil | scattering | as | like |

_____ red as blood, the rising sun

_____ the earth in light.

I watch it _____ on the lake,

_____ diamonds in its wake.

The air _____ alive with the song of birds,

_____ a well-trained choir, their voices merge,

And the mist that hangs like a _____ from the sky

Disappears in the blink of an eye.

Let's have fun!

Match the sentences below with the times at which the events are most likely to occur. Write the sentence number in the box beside the clock, and state whether the sentence contains a **simile**, **metaphor** or **personification**.

1. The sun disappeared below the horizon, like a ship sinking into the ocean. _____

2. The stars were jewels in the pre-dawn sky. _____

3. The clouds marched menacingly across the sky, threatening a late afternoon storm. _____

4. The first rays of light peeped shyly over the horizon. _____

5. Darkness covered the earth like a blanket. _____

6. The sun at midday was as bright as a silver coin. _____

Unit 18: Time

Let's have a test!

In questions 1–2, which sentence contains a simile?

1
- ○ Time is ancient.
- ○ The earth is as old as time.
- ○ The earth and time are old.
- ○ Time is an old man with a beard.

2
- ○ Last night I slept like a baby.
- ○ Last night the baby slept well.
- ○ Last night I slept well.
- ○ Last night I put the baby to sleep.

3 Which sentence contains a metaphor?
- ○ The sun is like a blazing fire.
- ○ The sun is as hot as a blazing fire.
- ○ The sun is a blazing fire in the sky.
- ○ The sun is like a fiery blaze.

In questions 4–5, which word completes the sentence correctly?

4 The night was _____ dark as chocolate.
- ○ has
- ○ is
- ○ like
- ○ as

5 The moon is rising _____ a big white balloon in the sky.
- ○ like
- ○ is
- ○ as
- ○ has

6 Which sentence contains an example of personification?
- ○ The wind blows every night.
- ○ The wind blew all night long.
- ○ The wind howled all night long.
- ○ The wind picked up during the night.

In questions 7–8, which option gives the subject in the sentence human qualities?

7 At night the moon _____ across the sky.
- ○ walks ○ shines ○ glows ○ flashes

8 The trees were _____ in the early morning breeze.
- ○ swaying ○ moving ○ bending ○ dancing

Let's write now!

Write a **poem** about time or something connected with it, like day or night. Use at least one **simile**, one **metaphor** and one example of **personification** in your poem.

108 Year 6 Grammar and Punctuation Workbook

Glossary of terms

Abbreviations are shortened forms of words or phrases, e.g. RSPCA, Mr.

Active voice is when the subject of the sentence performs the action, e.g. An earthquake destroyed the city.

Adjectives describe **nouns** and **pronouns**. Types of adjectives are:
- **comparing adjectives**, e.g. quieter, quietest
- **descriptive adjectives**, e.g. short, round, little, friendly
- **number adjectives**, e.g. some, many, four
- **ordering adjectives**, e.g. first, last
- **proper adjectives**, e.g. Australian, English.

Adverbs add meaning to verbs by telling how, where, when, how often and to what extent something is done, e.g. quickly, outside, yesterday, always, extremely.

Antonyms are words that are opposite in meaning, e.g. happy—sad.

Apostrophes are punctuation marks that show:
- where letters are missing when two words are joined to make one shorter word (a contraction), e.g. they're (they are)
- ownership; Jo's book (the book belonging to Jo).

Articles include the words **a**, **an** and **the**

Brackets ( ) are punctuation marks containing words that add information to sentences.

Clauses are groups of words that express a complete thought and contain a verb or verb group.

Colons (:) are punctuation marks that:
- show that more information is to follow
- are used after the names of the speakers in scripts or interviews.

Commas (,) are punctuation marks that:
- separate items in a list
- separate phrases and clauses from the rest of the sentence.

Commands are sentences that tell someone to do something. They usually end with a full stop (.) or sometimes an exclamation mark (!), e.g. Do your homework!

Conjunctions are words that connect other words, phrases and clauses in sentences, e.g. and, or, but.

Contractions are words formed when two words are joined to make one, shorter word, e.g. don't (do not).

Direct speech means the exact words that someone says, e.g. "I like school," he said.

Ellipses (…) are punctuation marks that show a pause in speech, e.g. Mmm … I think I understand.

Emotive language means language that causes an emotional response in people, e.g. The hunters massacred the herd of elephants.

Evaluative language means language that expresses an opinion, e.g. This is a good book.

Exclamations are sentences that express strong feelings. They end with an exclamation mark (!).

Indirect speech tells what other people said, without using their exact words, e.g. He said that he would try to help us.

Metaphors are figures of speech that directly compare one thing to something else, e.g. Time is a factory that churns out minutes and seconds.

Modality is when verbs and adverbs show how certain we are about something, e.g. might, definitely.

Nominalisation is turning verbs and adjectives into nouns, e.g. excite → excitement.

Nouns are naming words. There are several types of nouns:
- **Abstract nouns** name ideas and feelings; e.g. darkness, happiness.
- **Collective nouns** name groups of people, animals, places or things, e.g. herd, flock.
- **Common nouns** name general people, animals, places or things, e.g. girl, dog, country, car.

- **Proper nouns** name specific people, animals, places or things, e.g. Tom, Rover, Australia, Halloween.
- **Singular and plural nouns**, e.g. book → books.

Noun groups are groups of words that are built around a noun, e.g. The large brown <u>dog</u> with the long tail.

Passive voice means when the subject of the sentence has the action done to it, e.g. The city was destroyed by an earthquake.

Personification is when a metaphor gives animals and objects human qualities, e.g. The sun smiled down on the earth.

Phrases are groups of words that do not make sense on their own. They don't usually contain a verb, e.g. in the city, with long hair.

Prepositions are words that connect nouns, pronouns and phrases with other words in a sentence by telling where and when, e.g. in, on, from, since, until.

Pronouns are words that are used in place of nouns. These are:
- **demonstrative pronouns**, e.g. this, those
- **indefinite pronouns**, e.g. anyone, others
- **interrogative pronouns**, e.g. Who? What?
- **personal pronouns**, e.g. he, she
- **possessive pronouns**, e.g. his, her
- **reflexive pronouns**, e.g. myself, ourselves
- **relative pronouns**, e.g. that, which.

Questions are sentences that ask for information or opinions. They always end with a question mark (?).

Sentences are groups of words that make sense on their own. They always start with a capital letter and can end with a full stop, question mark or exclamation mark.
- **Simple sentences** contain only one verb.
- **Compound sentences** are two or more simple sentences that are joined together by a conjunction to form a single sentence.
- **Complex sentences** consist of at least one main clause and one or more dependent clauses.

Similes are figures of speech in which one thing is compared to something else unlike itself using the words *like* or *as*, e.g. The lake is like a mirror.

Speech marks are punctuation marks that are placed around spoken language, e.g. "Come here," said Mum.

Statements are sentences that give information or opinions. They always start with a capital letter and end with a full stop.

Subjects are the people, animals or things in a sentence that do the action.

Suffixes are groups of letters attached to the ends of words to change their meaning, e.g. bright, bright<u>er</u>, bright<u>ness</u>, bright<u>ly</u>.

Synonyms are words that are similar in meaning, e.g. talk, speak.

Tense shows when an action takes place—**present**, **past** or **future**, e.g. walk, walked, will walk.

Verbs are words that show what people, animals or things do. Types of verbs are:
- **being** and **having verbs**, e.g. is, was, has, had
- **doing verbs**, e.g. run, whispered, thought
- **helping verbs**, e.g. can, will.

verb groups are groups of words that are built around a verb, e.g. try to catch.

Answers

Unit 1 — Epic journeys

Let's find them! (pages 1–2)
1 deserts 2 Gobi Desert 3 father/uncle
4 Europeans 5 Venice 6 jewels/stories
7 Kublai Khan

Let's go to the next step! (page 2)
1 Santa Maria 2 Sahara 3 Niccolo 4 January
5 Bass Strait 6 Great Silk Road 7 Queensland

Let's aim high now! (page 2)
1 The **V**ikings, who came from **S**candinavia, sailed to **I**celand and **G**reenland.
2 In 1969 **N**eil **A**rmstrong, **B**uzz **A**ldrin and **M**ichael **C**ollins journeyed to the moon.
3 **C**hristopher **C**olumbus' three ships were the **N**ina, the **P**inta and the **S**anta **M**aria.
4 The botanist, **J**oseph **B**anks, accompanied **C**aptain **J**ames **C**ook on his first voyage.
5 The **N**orwegian, **T**hor **H**eyerdahl, sailed across the **P**acific **O**cean in a homemade raft.
6 **C**harles **D**arwin travelled to **B**razil, **A**ustralia, the **F**alkland **I**slands and the **G**alapagos **I**slands.
7 **T**here are many stories of epic journeys made by the ancient **G**reeks, **P**hoenicians, **E**gyptians and **R**omans.

Let's find them! (pages 3–4)
1 pods
2 clusters
3 party
4 welcome
5 disaster
6 conditions
7 starvation/exposure

Let's go to the next step! (page 4)
1 Early explorers often turned to the local population for help.
2 Many early explorers wrote of the difficulty of crossing vast mountain ranges.
3 Robert Scott, an officer in the navy, is famous for his exploration of Antarctica.
4 The caravan stopped at an oasis where the travellers could quench their thirst.
5 The sailors commented on the beauty of the island, with its clusters of palm trees.
6 Roald Amundsen's team of dogs contributed to his success in reaching the South Pole.
7 Robert Scott's first appointment was as a midshipman on the flagship of a squadron of battleships.

Let's aim high now! (page 4)
1 dangers 2 exhaustion 3 excitement
4 discoveries 5 death 6 preparations
7 knowledge

Let's put it together now! (page 5)
Matthew **F**linders was the first man to sail right around Australia. Amongst his **c**rew on the ship the *Investigator* was a botanist and two artist**s**. He started his circumnavigation of the continent at the southern tip of **W**estern Australia in 1801. He headed in an easterly direct**ion** until he came to Port Phillip. His first impress**ion** of the land around Melbourne was that it looked fertile. Even though his **s**hip was leaking badly, he completed his circumnavigation of Australia on 9th June 1803.

Let's have fun! (page 5)

	¹A	F	²G	H	³A	N	I	S	T	A	N
	R		O		D						
	M		L		⁴V	O	⁵Y	A	G	E	
	E		D		E		E				
	N				N		A			⁶G	
	I				⁷T	E	R	R	O	R	
⁸N	A	V	Y		U					O	
					R			⁹C	O	U	R	A	G	E
			¹⁰C	A	¹¹M	E	L			P	
					A						
					P						

Let's have a test! (page 6)
1 David Livingstone journeyed through Africa.
2 Cat
3 ocean
4 Amazon River

111

5 party, crew, army, band
6 committee
7 anxiety, loyalty, dedication, bravery
8 *ation*

Unit 2 A whale of a time!

Let's find them! (page 8)
Answers should include eight of the following: we, our, they, us, their, them, himself, he, it, me, you

Let's go to the next step! (page 8)
1 his 2 they 3 them/us 4 He 5 hers 6 its
7 her, she

Let's aim high now! (page 8)
1 myself 2 yourself/yourselves 3 itself
4 themselves 5 ourselves 6 herself 7 himself

Let's find them! (pages 9–10)
1 Who 2 someone 3 others 4 each 5 those
6 this 7 everyone 8 everything

Let's go to the next step! (page 10)
1 That/This 2 these 3 This 4 Which 5 Whose
6 What 7 Who

Let's aim high now! (page 10)
1 Someone 2 any 3 everything 4 none
5 anyone, no-one 6 something 7 both

Let's put it together now! (page 11)
"**Whose** bucket is **this**?" asked one of the village boys.
"It's **mine**," replied Myrna, "but **you** can use it." Myrna was exhausted. **She** watched as people tried to coax the whale back into the water. She asked **somebody** why it had beached **itself**, but he couldn't give her an answer.

Let's have fun! (page 11)
Stomach: him, us **Back:** ours, their
Tail: herself, themselves **Fin:** who, which
Jaw: this, those **Blowhole:** anyone, none

Let's have a test! (page 12)
1 They 2 our 3 themselves 4 Who 5 this
6 nothing 7 anyone 8 something, anything

Unit 3 Chocolate

Let's find them! (page 13)
1 smooth/sweet 2 cacao 3 sixteenth/nineteenth
4 dark brown 5 new 6 newly discovered 7 cocoa
8 edible

Let's go to the next step! (page 14)
liquid—solid
dark—light
expensive—cheap
coarse—smooth
natural—processed
patterned—plain
hard—soft
fresh—stale
curly—straight
hot—cold
flat—round
nutritious—unhealthy
interesting—boring
modern—traditional

Let's aim high now! (page 14)
1 colourful 2 famous 3 magical 4 friendly
5 foolish 6 homeless 7 basic

Let's find them! (pages 15–16)
1 most popular 2 darker 3 healthiest 4 lighter
5 sweeter 6 happier 7 smarter 8 most

Let's go to the next step! (page 16)

Adjective	Comparative	Superlative
smooth	smoother	smoothest
delicious	more delicious	most delicious
crunchy	**crunchier**	**crunchiest**
creamy	**creamier**	**creamiest**
expensive	**more/less expensive**	**most/least expensive**
good	**better**	**best**
rich	**richer**	**richest**
soft	**softer**	**softest**
fancy	**fancier**	**fanciest**
fresh	**fresher**	**freshest**
scrumptious	**more scrumptious**	**most scrumptious**
pretty	**prettier**	**prettiest**

Let's aim high now! (page 16)
1 crispier 2 largest 3 worst 4 most 5 better
6 more/less colourful 7 most wonderful

Let's put it together now! (page 17)
In 2011, a chocolate factory in England celebrated its 100th birthday in a very <u>tastier</u> way: it created the world's <u>larger</u> chocolate bar. The bar, which weighed 5827 kg, was almost 300 kg <u>heavy</u> than the previous record. The fifty people who worked on the project spent many <u>longer</u> hours carrying the mixture in buckets to the enormous mould. They said it was the <u>bigger</u>, <u>tiring</u>, but also the <u>enjoyable</u> challenge they had ever faced at the factory. Afterwards, the <u>hugest</u> bar was broken up and sold to raise money for charity.

Corrections: tasty, largest, heavier, long, biggest, most tiring, most enjoyable, huge

Let's have fun! (page 17)

Let's have a test! (page 18)
1 Chocolate is a delicious treat.
2 I put the chocolate in the fridge.
3 few
4 any
5 healthier
6 furthest
7 most hilarious
8 less popular

Unit 4 Shipwrecks

Let's find them! (page 20)
1 past 2 past 3 present 4 past 5 past 6 past
7 past 8 present

Let's go to the next step! (page 20)
The correct verbs are:
1 <u>lent</u> 2 <u>sank</u> 3 <u>explore</u> 4 <u>float</u> 5 <u>wanted</u>
6 <u>made</u> 7 <u>Remind</u>

Let's aim high now! (page 20)
1 He <u>saw</u> many shipwrecks.
2 She <u>wrote</u> about the *Titanic*.
3 I <u>thought</u> the shipwreck <u>was</u> over there.
4 Lots of people <u>climbed</u> into the lifeboat.
5 People <u>froze</u> to death in the icy water.
6 I <u>had</u> an interesting book about shipwrecks.
7 They <u>explored</u> the wrecks when they <u>went</u> to the island.

Let's find them! (pages 21–22)
1 can tell
2 was wrecked
3 was planning
4 to steal
5 were arrested
6 should be
7 Don't forget

Let's go to the next step! (page 22)
1 The divers <u>were hoping to find</u> the shipwreck.
2 They <u>had to abandon</u> the search for the wreck.
3 The octopus <u>had made</u> its home in the shipwreck.
4 They <u>have found</u> a chest of old coins in the wreck.
5 They <u>are going to explore</u> the old shipwreck tomorrow.
6 We <u>are going to watch</u> a documentary about the *Titanic*.
7 I <u>could make out</u> the shape of a hull through my goggles.

Let's aim high now! (page 22)
1 was/is 2 will 3 is/was 4 have/had
5 did, would 6 have/had 7 will/should

Answers 113

Let's put it together now (page 23)

In 1956 the Italian ship, the Andrea Doria, collide with another ship while on its way to New York. Although there was enough lifeboats on board, half of them couldn't been used because of the way the ship were listing. Luckily the ship stay afloat for 11 hours, which gave rescuers plenty of time to get to the vessel. These days, divers liked to look for treasure in and around the wreck of the Andrea Doria.

Corrections: collided, were, be, was, stayed, like

Let's have fun! (page 23)

Let's have a test! (page 24)

1. is
2. finds
3. are going
4. He sometimes seen the wreck.
5. forgotten
6. trying
7. does
8. have been

Unit 5 — We're going camping!

Let's find them! (page 26)

1. Dad is always full of beans in the morning.
2. Mum raised an eyebrow.
3. Chloe, my 14-year-old sister, rolled her eyes.
4. Since our outback adventure, she hasn't been able to enjoy her food.
5. I had enjoyed looking for dinosaur bones.
6. The red dust hadn't bothered me in the least.
7. "Where are we going, Dad?"

Let's go to the next step! (page 26)

1. I hate sleeping in a tent!
2. Park the camper van in that spot.
3. Have you ever been camping before?
4. Where are we going camping this year?
5. We go camping at least once every year.
6. Find out how long we can stay at the campsite.
7. Tonight we'll toast marshmallows around the campfire.

Let's aim high now! (page 26)

1. Wash your sleeping bag.
2. Keep the campsite clean.
3. Stay away from the campfire.
4. Help Dad pack away the tent.
5. Do not/Don't be a nuisance to other campers.
6. Do not/Don't make a noise late at night.
7. Find a campsite that is close to the sea.

Let's find them! (pages 27–28)

1. Chloe protested that they went camping last time.
2. I felt I had to defend Dad.
3. That time, we had stayed in luxury tents.
4. Then Dad dropped his next bombshell.
5. Mum couldn't believe the island had no running water!
6. Dad turned to his son.
7. Dad and the narrator thought it was a brilliant idea.

Let's go to the next step! (page 28)

Correct options:

1 The boys   2 is parking   3 go   4 belongs   5 live
6 Dad and I   7 Mum

Let's aim high now! (page 28)

The Australian flag is fluttering above the campsite.

The campsite was situated a long way from the beach.

Not all campsites have swimming pools.

The row of trees protects the tents in windy weather.

A family of ducks was swimming in the pond next to our campsite.

Our neighbours have bought a new campervan.

My uncle has got a big caravan.

Let's put it together now! (page 29)

The children **had** just arrived at the campsite when the storm started.

"How long do you think this will last**?**" asked Gabrielle.

"I'm not sure," replied the camp leader. "These storms can go on for a long time**.**"

He looked at Sammy, who **was** reading a book. "What **are** you reading, Sammy**?**" he asked. Sammy held up the book. "It's by my favourite author," he said. "My friends and I **love** his books."

Let's have fun! (page 29)

1. How many times have you been camping?
2. How amazing was that camping trip!
3. Show us where your caravan is parked.
4. I really enjoy going on camping trips.
5. Which campsite are you staying at?

Let's have a test! (page 30)

1. Where are you going camping this year?
2. .
3. Wait in the caravan.
4. Listen
5. The lady in the caravan
6. are going
7. is, Does
8. that

Unit 6   Courage

Let's find them! (pages 31–32)

1 adjective   2 adjective   3 adjective   4 adjective
5 adjective   6 verb   7 verb

Let's go to the next step! (page 32)

1 growing   2 charred   3 broken   4 missing
5 crumbling   6 pleased, punishing
7 freezing, stranded

Let's aim high now! (page 32)

1 crying   2 scared   3 rewarding   4 terrifying
5 written   6 exhausted   7 fighting

Let's find them! (pages 33–34)

1 defending   2 sailing   3 Training   4 jumping
5 walking   6 swimming   7 riding

Let's go to the next step! (page 34)

1. Bullying is not something to be proud of.
2. Hurdling requires a lot of skill and training.
3. Supporting good causes is one of his hobbies!
4. Diving to great depths requires great courage.
5. Overcoming obstacles can make you stronger.
6. Reporting bad behaviour sometimes takes courage.
7. Protecting the environment is very important to him.

Let's aim high now! (page 34)

1 caring   2 treating   3 flying   4 sprinting
5 debating   6 coaching   7 cycling

Let's put it together now! (page 35)

People who perform acts of bravery, like **rushing** into **burning** buildings to save those **trapped** inside, or **working** to help **starving**/**orphaned** or **orphaned**/**starving** children in **war-torn** countries, are true heroes who deserve our respect.

Let's have fun (page 35)

x	l	t	v	o	l	u	n	t	e	e	r	i	n	g
c	e	x	v	w	q	h	y	r	e	s	c	u	e	d
t	a	b	a	s	s	d	j	f	n	d	z	n	f	d
n	r	j	h	g	n	e	y	l	f	e	r	g	j	k
r	n	r	w	c	n	r	f	h	j	y	z	n	m	o
u	i	q	v	a	q	u	h	j	d	s	h	i	i	k
b	n	t	i	h	g	j	h	s	h	e	g	y	g	d
a	g	j	n	n	z	n	n	v	s	n	w	r	r	t
g	n	i	h	c	t	i	w	h	h	i	k	t	c	x
a	g	n	i	r	e	e	n	i	a	t	n	u	o	m
z	y	d	e	t	e	l	p	m	o	c	u	h	d	a

Let's have a test! (page 36)

1. challenging
2. relieved
3. threatening
4. embarrassed
5. Believing
6. complaining
7. Focusing, doing
8. Dreaming, succeeding

Unit 7 Greek mythology

Let's find them! (pages 37–38)
2 had hoped 3 was thrown 4 had hidden
5 used 6 fought 7 found

Let's go to the next step! (page 38)
1 hesitantly 2 always/occasionally 3 Fortunately
4 angrily 5 instantly 6 occasionally/always
7 inside

Let's aim high now! (page 38)
1 anywhere—place
2 tonight—time
3 early—time
4 menacingly—manner
5 often—frequency
6 anxiously—manner
7 quite—degree

Let's find them! (pages 39–40)
1 more radiantly 2 more lustrously
3 very angry 4 harder 5 more kindly

Let's go to the next step (page 40)
Correct options:
1 incredibly 2 too 3 so 4 extremely 5 very
6 rather 7 overly

Let's aim high now! (page 40)

Adverb	Comparative	Superlative
hard	harder	hardest
early	earlier	earliest
easily	more easily	most easily
high	higher	highest
carefully	more/less carefully	most/least carefully
comfortably	more comfortably	most comfortably
soon	sooner	soonest
often	more often	most often
late	later	latest
enthusiastically	more enthusiastically	most enthusiastically
far	further	furthest
curiously	more curiously	most curiously
fast	faster	fastest
efficiently	more/less efficiently	most/least efficiently

Let's put it together now! (page 41)
King Minos had imprisoned the inventor, Daedalus, and his son, Icarus, in a **very** high tower next to the labyrinth. Birds **often** perched on the window ledge, and when Daedalus noticed some feathers drifting into the tower, he **immediately** thought of a way of escaping. He told Icarus to collect the feathers. Meanwhile, he worked **more enthusiastically** than he had ever worked before fashioning a pair of wings for himself and his son. He used the wax from their candles to hold the feathers together. When the wings were **finally** ready, father and son strapped them on. Daedalus warned his son that the **higher** he flew, the more dangerous it would be. Daedalus did not heed his father's warning and flew **too** close to the sun. The wax on his wings melted and he plunged into the sea.

Let's have fun! (page 41)
1 lou**dly**
2 of**ten**
3 rath**er**
4 **m**ore crue**lly**
5 **e**arly
6 incre**dibly**
7 m**o**st **c**are**fully**
8 **v**ery

Let's have a test! (page 42)
1 Theseus always tried to help his people.
2 Theseus had seen the Minotaur before.
3 Athena was standing nearby.
4 Icarus acted recklessly.
5 quite
6 extremely
7 higher
8 sooner

Unit 8 Chew on this!

Let's find them! (pages 43–44)
1 but 2 when 3 and 4 If 5 after 6 or 7 because

Let's go to the next step! (page 44)
1 after 2 Once 3 because 4 but 5 so 6 until 7 if

Let's aim high now! (page 44)
Cross out these conjunctions:
1 until 2 nor 3 yet 4 whereas 5 although 6 if
7 unless

116 Year 6 Grammar and Punctuation Workbook

Let's find them! (page 45)
1 of **2** in **3** to **4** on **5** by **6** for **7** at

Let's go to the next step! (page 46)
1 under **2** near **3** during **4** through, in
5 against, for **6** past, on, from **7** to, since, of

Let's aim high now! (page 46)
Cross out these prepositions:
1 down **2** to **3** since **4** without **5** off **6** except
7 through

Let's put it together now (page 47)
Most people can lift very light objects with their teeth, **but** some people have incredibly strong teeth and can lift much heavier loads. A man **from** India, known as the Tooth Warrior **or** The Man with the Diamond Teeth, can lift a bicycle with his teeth! Another man recently broke the world record **for** carrying the heaviest load the longest distance using only his teeth! He clenched a table weighing 12 kg **between** his jaws **and** carried it for almost 12 m. To add to the table's weight, a girl weighing 50 kg sat **on** it!

Let's have fun! (page 47)
Conjunctions (upper jaw): after, and, but, so, nor, if, or, yet, until, unless, while, when, because, either, once, although
Prepositions (lower jaw): at, to, in, on, over, up, for, by, with, during, from, without, into, about, along, near

Let's have a test! (page 48)
1 when **2** and **3** because **4** but **5** with **6** on
7 for **8** from

Unit 9 Striking it rich!

Let's find them! (pages 49–50)
1 adjective **2** adverb **3** adjective **4** adverb
5 adverb **6** adverb **7** adjective

Let's go to the next step! (page 50)
1. Australia exports gold <u>around the world.</u> adverbial
2. The gold bars were delivered <u>to the bank.</u> adverbial
3. The opals <u>in the box</u> were blue and green. adjectival
4. The diamond necklace cost a lot <u>of money.</u> adjectival
5. The gold nugget was lying <u>beside the stream.</u> adverbial
6. My mother bought an opal ring <u>from that shop.</u> adverbial
7. The treasures <u>beneath the earth</u> are often hard to find. adjectival

Let's aim high now! (page 50)
1. in her ring—adjectival
2. for a mining company—adverbial
3. for many days—adverbial
4. from the mine—adjectival
5. without a price tag—adjectival
6. inside a safe—adverbial
7. from falling rocks—adverbial

Let's find them! (pages 51–52)
1. Life on the goldfields
2. Living on the goldfields
3. more permanent dwellings of wood, bark and canvas
4. thriving towns and cities
5. picks, shovels and any other equipment they needed
6. on horseback, by cart or on foot
7. wood, bark and canvas
8. stores, hotels and theatres

Let's go to the next step! (page 52)
1. Gold, silver and platinum are precious metals.
2. In winter it was cold, wet and windy on the goldfields.
3. The miners bought meat, milk, eggs and vegetables from a local farmer.
4. A lady wearing a diamond necklace, bracelet and earrings came to see us.
4. People from Europe, Asia, Africa and America came to the Australian goldfields.
5. While digging for opals, the miner found some old coins, bones and bits of metal.
7. The jeweller showed me a ring set with diamonds, rubies, emeralds and sapphires.

Let's aim high now! (page 52)
2. The boat from Europe carried supplies for the gold mines.
3. Some lucky fortune hunters found large amounts of gold.
4. The raging bushfire destroyed the miners' huts.

Answers   117

5   The famous jeweller designed a beautiful gold necklace.
6   The new gold mine provides work for many people.
7   The heat from the furnace caused the gold to melt.

Let's put it together now! (page 53)

Early **gold** miners used a pan to extract gold **from** streams and dry riverbeds. They would scoop up some gravel**,** add a bit of water and then move the pan about gently. The gold would sink **to** the bottom. Some old gold **mines** have become tourist attractions where people can experience what life was like for those early diggers. Visitors are shown how to pan for gold. They are even allowed to keep any flakes **of** gold that they might find. I have a bottle with two little flakes of gold **in** it!

Let's have fun! (page 53)

a box of jewels—necklaces, rings and earrings
energy from fossil fuels—coal, oil and gas
a bracelet with gemstones—diamonds, rubies and sapphires
savings in the bank—dollars, cents and pounds

Let's have a test! (page 54)

1   of gold coins
2   in her collection
3   to a jeweller
4   between the mine
5   We get energy from coal, oil and gas.
6   Crystals, precious stones, precious metals and fossil fuels come from the earth.
7   He bought a large, round barrel of oil.
8   A, with

Unit 10   Natural disasters

Let's find them! (pages 55–56)

1   Dorothea McKellar
2   Tropical cyclones in the north
3   Heavy rainfall
4   forests and human settlements
5   the weather patterns that cause these natural disasters
6   houses
7   instructions to evacuate our homes

Let's go to the next step! (page 56)

1 verb   2 subject   3 object   4 object   5 object
6 verb   7 subject

Let's aim high now! (page 56)

1   The rising waters covered (our garden).
2   The wild winds blew down (power lines).
3   The bushfire scorched (our neighbour's fence).
4   The large wave carried away (cars and houses).
5   The rumbling volcano frightened (the townspeople).
6   The fire destroyed (the habitats of birds and other wildlife).
7   A hailstone the size of a tennis ball broke (one of our windows).

Let's find them! (pages 57–58)

1 passive   2 passive   3 passive   4 active   5 active
6 passive   7 passive

Let's go to the next step! (page 58)

1 are being   2 will be   3 were   4 been
5 was/is being   6 to be   7 had been

Let's aim high now! (page 58)

1   Cars were lifted into the air by the tornado.
2   The bushfire was caused by a lightning strike.
3   Our holiday was cut short by the heavy rains.
4   The farmers' crops were destroyed by cyclones.
5   The dents in our car were caused by large hailstones.

Let's put it together now! (page 59)

On 22nd February 2011, the city of Christchurch **was** hit by a 6.3 magnitude earthquake. It **caused** widespread damage because it occurred so close to the city. Altogether, 185 people **were killed**, making it the second worst natural disaster in New Zealand's history. It has also **been** very expensive to repair the damage caused by the earthquake.

When the earthquake **struck**, many people **came** to the aid of those who **were** trapped, including ordinary citizens.

Let's have fun! (page 59)

1 destroyed   2 islands   3 screams   4 animals
5 streets   6 tsunami   7 earthquake   8 ripped

Let's have a test! (page 60)
1. It get worse every month.
2. blown
3. The houses near the river
4. the small island
5. The flagpole was blown down by the wind.
6. by the earthquake
7. have been hurt
8. were destroyed by

Unit 11 Robots

Let's find them! (pages 61–62)
1. "What do you mean**?**" asked Jacqui.
2. "It's good that robots are able to do boring or dangerous jobs**,**" said Dad.
3. "You mean like the robot they've sent to Mars**,**" interrupted Jacqui.
4. "Exactly**!**" exclaimed Dad.
5. "But on the other hand, robots are putting people out of work**.**"
6. "So**,**" mused Jacqui, "robots are like … what's that saying again**?**"
7. "Like a double-edged sword**,**" said Dad. "They have their good points and their bad points**.**"

Let's go to the next step! (page 62)
1. "Is this robot powered by batteries?" asked Paul.
2. "If only I had a robot to carry out the garbage," whined Rory.
3. "One good thing about robots," said Joe, "is that they never get sick!"
4. "This robot is made from metal and plastic," said the science teacher.
5. "If you want to know how to build a robot," said Neil, "watch this video."
6. "I think that people who can build robots are very clever," commented Aunt Maud.
7. "One problem with robots is that they are unable to think for themselves," said Will, "but maybe that's a good thing."

Let's aim high now! (page 62)
1. "Many science fiction books are about robots**,**" said Mr Marks.
2. "Have you ever built a robot**?**" asked Jules, "because I haven't**.**"
3. "Look what I made in robotics**!**" exclaimed Olivia, holding up a small robot.
4. "I went to see the movie about robots**,**" announced Hilda, "and it was scary**.**"
5. The teacher said, "Many robots are used in factories to build things like cars**.**"
6. The boss exclaimed, "The best thing about robots is that they never complain**!**"
7. "I think robots can really help humans**,**" said Ms Scott, "as long as we use them properly**.**"

Let's find them! (page 63)
1. He said that he built his first robot using a kit he bought in a hobby shop.
2. He said the instructions were very easy to follow.
3. He explained to us how he put the parts together and programmed the robot.
4. I asked him how long it took him to build the robot.
5. Dave replied that the first one took him a few days to put together.
6. He added that he'd built two more robots since then.
7. These, he said, had taken him much less time to make.

Let's go to the next step! (page 64)
Cross out these verbs:
1. can 2. have 3. will, wants 4. has 5. sees 6. shall
7. is

Let's aim high now! (page 64)
1. she loved playing with her robot
2. it was her brother's robot
3. he wanted a robot for his birthday
4. he didn't know how to build a robot
5. they wouldn't finish the robot today
6. he had learnt how to program a robot
7. which robot he was going to buy

Let's put it together now! (page 65)
"Mum, if you could buy a robot to help you around the house, would you get one**?**" asked Kevin.
Mum replied that she had never really thought about it, but probably **would**, if it wasn't too expensive.
"Which jobs would you get the robot to do?" asked Kevin.
"Well**,**" replied Mum, "the first thing I'd program it to do would be to clean your room**!**" Kevin said that **was** fine with him.

Answers 119

Let's have fun! (page 65)
"Would you like to own a robot?" asked Mervyn. Nina said that she would like a robot that would do her homework for her.

Let's have a test! (page 66)
1 "Are robots fun to play with?" asked Stuart.
2 "This is my new robot," said Jake, "and that's my old one."
3 Dad exclaimed, "What a magnificent robot!"
4 "That robot scares me," said Jill.
5 was
6 would
7 should, my
8 would, their

Unit 12 Animals with armour

Let's find them! (pages 67–68)
1 simple sentence
2 compound sentence
3 compound sentence
4 compound sentence
5 simple sentence
6 simple sentence

Let's go to the next step! (page 68)
1 yet 2 nor 3 but 4 or 5 so 6 and 7 but

Let's aim high now! (page 68)
1 Birds have scales on their legs and on their heads.
2 Most fish have scales for protection, but early fish had hard, bony plates.
3 Hedgehogs sleep under bushes and/or in holes in the ground.
4 The tortoise felt threatened by the dog, so/and it retreated into its shell.
5 Hedgehogs are mainly nocturnal, yet/but they can be active during the day.
6 Some dinosaurs had spikes on their bodies, but/and others were covered in plates.
7 The echidna came out of the burrow and started walking towards us.

Let's find them! (pages 69–70)
1 dependent clause
2 main clause
3 dependent clause
4 dependent clause
5 main clause
6 dependent clause

Let's go to the next step! (page 70)
1 When I approached it
2 once I've fed my pet turtle
3 Although the snake is harmless
4 which is very small
5 If you see a saltwater crocodile on the river bank
6 because it was too small
7 with whom I watched the documentary

Let's aim high now! (page 70)
1 [If a lobster loses a claw or leg], [it will grow a new one].
2 The porcupine, [whose body is covered in spines], is a rodent.
3 [The tortoise won't emerge from its shell] [while it feels threatened].
4 [I saw a large saltwater crocodile] [when I went to the Northern Territory].
5 The crocodile, [which was enormous], suddenly jumped out of the water.
6 [Yesterday I met a man] [who had been attacked by a saltwater crocodile].
7 [Before we visited the reptile park], [I watched a documentary about crocodiles].

Let's put it together now! (page 71)
Hermit crabs, **which** have soft bodies, use the shells of other animals for protection. **If/When** they find an empty shell, they climb right into it **and** drag it around with them. **Because** the shell doesn't grow with them, they go through several of these 'mobile homes' in a lifetime.
There is strong competition for shells among hermit crabs. **If/When** they see a crab with what they think is a better shell, a few of them will cooperate to pull the shell away. Then they turn on each other and the one who comes out on top gets the shell!
Hermit crabs make great pets, **but** people don't always know how to look after them. Crabs are often kept in enclosures which are too small **or** are made from unsuitable materials. Glass tanks with a secure screen cover are the best form of housing.

Let's have fun! (page 71)
Seahorse—I look like a mammal, but I'm really a fish. compound
Porcupine—My quills, which are very sharp, protect me from predators. OR
My quills, which protect me from predators, are very sharp. complex
Dinosaur—I became extinct millions of years ago. simple

Let's have a test! (page 72)
1. A rhino beetle is large, but a rhino is larger.
2. yet
3. and
4. nor
5. who
6. unless
7. that
8. The rhino, which I saw at the zoo, is a large animal with a thick skin.

Unit 13 Famous Australians

Let's find them! (pages 73–74)
1. 'All One Race'
2. 'Father Sky and Mother Earth'
3. 'Stradbroke Dreamtime'
4. 'Little Fella'
5. 'The Rainbow Serpent'
6. 'The Fringe Dwellers'

Let's go to the next step! (page 74)
1. 'Ballad of **the** Drover'.
2. 'Waltzing Matilda**'**.
3. '**The** Man from Snowy River'.
4. 'Sydney **Morning** Herald'
5. 'Neighbours'**'**.
6. Australians**:**
7. films**:**

Let's aim high now! (page 74)
1. The documentary, 'A Very Short War', is about a famous Australian pilot.
2. Dorothea McKellar wrote a famous poem about Australia called 'My Country'.
3. The conservationist, Ian Kiernan, has co-authored a book called 'Coming Clean'.
4. John Marsden's book, 'Tomorrow, When the War Began', has been made into a film.
5. Australia's national anthem, 'Advance Australia Fair'**,** was composed by Peter Dodds McCormick.
6. These are my favourite books by John Marsden**:** 'Tomorrow, When the War Began' and 'The Other Side of Dawn'.
7. These are my three favourite poems by Oodgeroo**:** 'Muncipal Gum', 'Understand Old One' and 'We Are Going'.

Let's find them! (pages 75–76)
1. (ophthalmologist)
2. (a country in north-west Africa)
3. (established in 1992)
4. UK
5. NT
6. NSW
7. New Zealand

Let's go to the next step! (page 76)
1. Oodgeroo Noonuccal **(**1920–1993**)** is a famous Australian poet.
2. Banjo Paterson lived on a property of 40 000 acres **(**160 km²**)** near Yass.
3. Sir Donald George Bradman **(**The Don**)** had a test batting average of 99.94 runs.
4. Fred Hollows **(**born in New Zealand**)** did most of his work in Australia, Africa and Asia.
5. Dawn Fraser **(**AO MBE**)** was the first woman to swim 100 m freestyle in under a minute.
6. Doctor Victor Chang **(**born Chang Yam Him**)** was a pioneer of heart transplantation in Australia.
7. Nobel Prize winner Howard Florey **(**1898–1968**)** studied medicine at the University of Adelaide.

Let's aim high now! (page 76)
1. Some Australian actors live in Los Angeles in California. LA
2. Hugh Jackman was born in Perth, the capital of Western Australia. WA
3. A number of Australians have received the Victoria Cross for bravery. VC
4. The governor-general is making an important announcement at 4 o'clock. pm
5. The prime minister's official residence is in the Australian Capital Territory. ACT
6. Many Australian and New Zealand Army Corps soldiers died at Gallipoli in 1915. ANZAC

Answers

7 Neville Bonner, Australia's first Aboriginal senator, died in Ipswich in Queensland in 1999. Qld

Let's put it together now! (page 77)

Dame Joan Sutherland (1926–2010) was born in Sydney and went on to become one of the greatest opera singers in the world. She had a strong voice and got a lucky break when she won free singing lessons at the age of 19. Her dream was to become an opera star, and in 1951 she went to the UK, where she met and married the Australian pianist, Richard Bonynge (pronounced Boning). Among the many famous operas in which she sang the female lead were the following: 'The Magic Flute', 'Suor Angelica' and 'Hamlet'. She retired in 1990.

Let's have fun (page 77)

1 Cate Blanchett, Russell Crowe and Hugh Jackman.
2 Liesel Jones, Lleyton Hewitt and Cadel Evans.
3 Julia Gillard, Kevin Rudd and John Howard.
4 (nicknamed the Thorpedo)
5 (1897–1935)
6 (published in 2001)
7 TAS
8 Ave
9 PO

Let's have a test! (page 78)

1 Donald Bradman wrote a book called 'My Cricketing Life'.
2 This week the TV program 'An Australian Story' is about a famous actor.
3 My favourite poem by Henry Lawson is 'The Ballad of the Drover'.
4 These men are Australian authors: Patrick White and John Marsden.
5 born in 1942
6 UNEP
7 SMS
8 vs

Unit 14 Acting it out

Let's find them! (page 80)

1 which
2 who
3 whose
4 Although
5 whenever
6 because
7 when

Let's go to the next step! (page 80)

1 Once the curtain went up, the actor started to relax.
2 The play, which recently won an award, was very funny.
3 Before I go on stage, I always have butterflies in my tummy.
4 The actors, who had been rehearsing all day, were exhausted.
5 Although I enjoy watching plays, I would rather go to the movies.
6 When you go to the theatre, make sure you have your ticket with you!
7 The director, whose parents had been famous actors, was trying to make a name for himself.

Let's aim high now! (page 80)

1 if this one is a success. adverbial
2 after I had read the book. adverbial
3 because we arrived late. adverbial
4 who is still very young/whose latest play is due to open soon adjectival
5 whose latest play is due to open soon/who is still very young adjectival
6 which I have yet to see adjectival
7 since I went with the school last year adverbial

Let's find them! (pages 81–82)

1 Stallholder: Mmm … that's a shame.
2 a good dollop of sense (hands her the card marked 'sense')
3 Melissa: (looking uncertain)
4 Stallholder: Of course it will … trust me. (Turns to Lenny)

122   Year 6 Grammar and Punctuation Workbook

Let's go to the next step! (page 82)
1 Rich lady:
2 (smacking his lips)
3 Fairies:
4 (falling over her feet)
5 Let me think …
6 (Moves towards the Athletes' Stall)
7 Mmmm …

Let's aim high now! (page 82)
1 Shopkeeper: (turning to customer) Will that be all, Madam?
2 Crier: (moving to centre stage) Words for sale! Words for sale!
3 Melissa: (shouting from her room) Mum, where's … oh, never mind.
4 Customer: (taking out her wallet) Yes, that's all for now, thank you.
5 Lady: (looking surprised) What on … I don't believe it! My wallet is empty!
6 Twinkletoes: (walking towards Fairy Stall) I wonder what we'll find here?
7 Fairy: Oh, that's much better. (Starts dancing about) I can dance again!

Let's put it together now! (page 83)
Goblin #1: (turning to the other goblins) Have you noticed that I haven't been as mean as usual lately?
Goblin #2: Now that you mention it, I haven't felt like annoying anyone all week.
Goblin #3: (looking thoughtful) Mmmm … now that's interesting. I haven't been nearly as horrible as I normally am.
Goblin #1: If you ask me, it's high time we did something about it!

Let's have fun (page 83)
Teacher: (looking irritable) Jimmy, unless you stop talking and start doing some work, you'll be spending recess with me.
Jimmy: I'm trying to do my work … really I am. It's just this tongue of mine that won't stop moving.

Let's have a test! (page 84)
1 whose
2 unless
3 , which
4 , although
5 Doctor: Take some of this (hands her the medicine) and you'll soon feel better.

6 Lady: (scratching around in her bag) Now where … oh, here it is!
7 Peter: (moving forward) Is this what you're looking for?
8 Zoe: (looking confused) But … No! I don't believe it!

Unit 15 Changing fashions

Let's find them! (page 86)
1 I'll 2 He's 3 who'll 4 Papa's 5 wouldn't 6 I've
7 It's 8 I'm

Let's go to the next step! (page 86)
1 I don't think I'd have liked wearing a curly wig.
2 She doesn't know what people wore a hundred years ago.
3 I wanted to try on the old breeches, but they wouldn't let me.
4 They're going to buy him a new outfit that's more fashionable.
5 I haven't seen the movie, but I believe the costumes are magnificent.
6 He didn't want to wear the fancy hat, but his sister said it'd make him look cool.
7 We aren't going to the dress-up party because we won't be here that weekend.

Let's aim high now! (page 86)
1 Who is—Who's
2 does not—doesn't
3 must not—mustn't, do not—don't
4 mother is—mother's
5 should have—should've
6 sister is—sister's, cannot—can't
7 We have—We've, he will—he'll, will not—won't

Let's find them! (page 87)
1 fashions 2 fashions 3 help 4 reports 5 skin
6 clothes 7 next idea

Let's go to the next step! (page 88)
1 sheep's 2 glove's 3 king's 4 people's
5 dresses' 6 Crocodiles' 7 friend's

Let's aim high now! (page 88)
1 The dress's bodice is made of satin.
2 Lady Gaga's outfits are often outrageous.
3 The singers' costumes were very colourful.

4   The garment's buttons are shaped like pearls.
5   The teachers' clothes are very old-fashioned.
6   The new student's hair has been cut in the latest style.
7   You can buy the designers' collections at the new store.

Let's put it together now! (page 89)

I can't believe it! My brother's latest thing is to wear his pants so that most of his undies are showing! He thinks it's cool. I don't. Mum's pleas and Dad's harsh words have fallen on deaf ears. Today he wanted me to go to the shops with him. I told him I'd rather eat worms.

Let's have fun (page 89)

2 you're 3 I'd 4 fashion's 5 we're 6 mightn't
7 they're 8 you'd 9 boy's 10 children's
11 woman's 12 athletes' 13 princes'

Let's have a test! (page 90)

1   Moira isn't wearing her new outfit.
2   They'll, they've
3   would've, it's
4   children's, stores
5   will not
6   The dress's hem has come loose.
7   I found this shirt in the men's department.
8   baby's

Unit 16 Rules and regulations

Let's find them! (pages 91–92)

1 low 2 high 3 low 4 low 5 low 6 high 7 high

Let's go to the next step! (page 92)

1   could—uncertainty
2   will not—certainty
3   always—certainty
4   must—certainty
5   probably—uncertainty
6   may not—uncertainty
7   definitely—certainty

Let's aim high now! (page 92)
Correct words:
1 may 2 might not 3 must 4 must not
5 Perhaps 6 positively 7 definitely

Let's find them! (page 93)

1 organisation 2 protection 3 responsibility
4 behaviour 5 importance 6 confusion 7 safety

Let's go to the next step! (page 94)

2   secu**rit**y
3   popul**at**ion
4   childish**ness**
5   entr**ance**
6   forgetful**ness**
7   fatal**ity**
8   resist**ance**
9   explos**ion**
10 visib**ility**
11 insur**ance**
12 friend**liness**
13 interrup**tion**
14 accept**ance**

Let's aim high now! (page 94)

1 service 2 information 3 enforcement
4 statement 5 procedure 6 approval 7 pollution

Let's put it together now! (page 95)

The council wants to make our local park a dog-friendly area, where dogs no longer have to be leashed. I am **definitely** against this idea. It will place both the dogs and the people who use the park in **danger**. Some dogs **could/might** run off and end up on a busy road, or they **might/could** hurt a young child. Parks are for people. They are for **recreation** and **relaxation**. People don't want to be bothered by strange animals sniffing around their picnic lunch, or interfering with their games. I am happy to share the park with dogs, as long as they are on a leash. Come on, Councillors! Where is your sense of **responsibility**?

Let's have fun (page 95)

preparatio**n**, revisi**o**n, re**f**usal, s**i**ght, a**g**reement, thoug**ht**, crea**t**ion, bel**ief**, decisio**n**, ju**dg**ement
Rule: No fighting

Let's have a test! (page 96)
1 He must have broken the law.
2 He will definitely get a fine.
3 They might make it a rule.
4 I sometimes obey the rules.
5 imprisonment
6 alertness
7 The jury has come to a decision.
8 ment

Unit 17 Television

Let's find them! (pages 97–98)
1 most amazing 2 informative 3 interesting
4 enjoyable 5 relaxing 6 tiring 7 violent
8 boring

Let's go to the next step! (page 98)
1 poor—negative
2 superb—positive
3 dull—negative
4 clumsy—negative
5 popular—positive
6 happy—positive
7 outstanding—positive

Let's aim high now! (page 98)
1 <u>Modern</u>, <u>flat</u>—fact
2 <u>funny</u>—opinion
3 <u>beautiful</u>—opinion
4 <u>interesting</u>—opinion
5 <u>Australian</u>—fact
6 <u>Some</u>, <u>young</u>—fact
7 <u>Wildlife</u>, <u>more entertaining</u>, <u>reality</u>—opinion

Let's find them! (pages 99–100)
1 defenceless 2 poisoned 3 noxious 4 ancient
5 destroyed 6 fragile 7 crimes

Let's go to the next step! (page 100)
More emotive words:
1 raced 2 skyrocketed 3 crushed 4 ripped
5 stampeded 6 mob, hurled 7 savaged

Let's aim high now! (page 100)
1 funny—hilarious
2 frightened—terrified
3 tired—exhausted
4 man—criminal
5 cross—furious
6 pleased—overjoyed
7 pain—agony

Let's put it together now! (page 101)
I agree that some television programs are **unsuitable** for young people. However, there are also lots of **excellent** shows that give us **important** information. For instance, last night I watched a program about the **devastating** effects of global warming on the Arctic region. Apparently, the ice is melting at an **alarming** rate, and experts **fear** that the people, wildlife and plants in the area are at **risk**.

Let's have fun (page 101)
1 Ambitious young athletes will find this program inspiring. *Diary of a Future Champion*
2 Teens will love this exciting new adventure series. *A Wild Ride*!
3 This is an informative, if somewhat dull, program about the discovery of gold in Australia. *In Search of a Fortune*
4 Not too many people will be enthralled by this new version of a famous fairy tale. *Cinderella Goes to Hollywood*
5 Some people might find the images in this new wildlife series distressing. *The Hunters*
6 This heart-warming story explores the special relationship between humans and their pets. *My Best Friend*
7 Join us on this amazing journey into an artist's strange world. *Colour My World*

Let's have a test! (page 102)
1 Their television set is ugly.
2 wonderful
3 That program is new.
4 entertaining
5 Vandals wrecked the cameraman's equipment.
6 surging
7 revolting
8 icy

Answers 125

Unit 18 Time

Let's find them! (pages 103–104)
1–4 Similes:
Time is like the rain
Time is like a drummer
Time is like a wheel
Time can be as cruel as a tyrant
Time can be as quiet as a cat
Time can be as loud as thunder
5–7 Metaphors:
Time is a furnace
Time is a river
Time is a disappearing act

Let's go to the next step! (page 104)
1. the wind
2. the earth
3. a feather
4. a snail
5. two sharp needles
6. a ruler
7. a bird

Let's aim high now! (page 104)
1. money
2. a gift
3. bridge
4. music
5. a rollercoaster ride
6. at a donkey's pace
7. the slow passage

Let's find them! (page 105)
1. stand still
2. race
3. crawl
4. give a wake-up call
5. has hands
6. has a face
7. strides

Let's go to the next step! (page 106)
Option that personifies:
1 crept   2 embraced   3 rushed   4 angrily   5 hid
6 forgot to   7 smiled

Let's aim high now! (page 106)
1. Time won't <u>wait</u> for you, so you'd better hurry up!
2. My alarm clock <u>screams</u> in my ear every morning.
3. The clock <u>announced</u> that it was time for me to leave.
4. The sun <u>wakes up</u> at dawn to <u>rule</u> the world once more.
5. Time <u>gobbles up</u> the minutes, but <u>eats</u> the hours more slowly.
6. The shadows <u>stretched forth their arms</u> as the afternoon wore on.
7. My alarm clock <u>reminds</u> me every morning that I have to go to school.

Let's put it together now! (page 107)
<u>As</u> red as blood, the rising sun
<u>Bathes</u> the earth in light.
I watch it <u>dancing</u> on the lake,
<u>Scattering</u> diamonds in its wake.

The air <u>is</u> alive with the song of birds,
<u>Like</u> a well-trained choir, their voices merge,
And the mist that hangs like a <u>veil</u> from the sky
Disappears in the blink of an eye.

Let's have fun (page 107)
1. 7 pm The sun disappeared below the horizon, like a ship sinking into the ocean. <u>simile</u>
2. 3:30 am The stars were jewels in the pre-dawn sky. <u>metaphor</u>
3. 4:30 pm The clouds marched menacingly across the sky, threatening a late afternoon storm. <u>personification</u>
4. 5:30 am The first rays of light peeped shyly over the horizon. <u>personification</u>
5. 10 pm Darkness covered the earth like a blanket. <u>simile</u>
6. 11:59 am The sun at midday was as bright as a silver coin. <u>simile</u>

Let's have a test! (page 108)
1. The earth is as old as time.
2. Last night I slept like a baby.
3. The sun is a blazing fire in the sky.
4. as
5. like
6. The wind howled all night long.
7. walks
8. dancing